The Dialogic Curriculum

The Dialogic Curriculum
Teaching and Learning
in a Multicultural Society

Patricia Lambert Stock

Department of English
Michigan State University

Foreword by
Maxine Greene

Boynton/Cook Publishers
HEINEMANN
Portsmouth, NH

Boynton/Cook Publishers
A subsidiary of Reed Elsevier Inc.
361 Hanover Street
Portsmouth, NH 03801-3912

Offices and agents throughout the world

We would like to thank those who have given their permission to include material in this book. Every effort has been made to contact the copyright holders for permission to reprint borrowed material where necessary. We regret any oversights that may have occurred and would be happy to rectify them in future printings of this work.

Library of Congress Cataloging-in-Publication Data
Stock, Patricia L.
    The dialogic curriculum: teaching and learning in a multicultural
society / Patricia Lambert Stock.
        p.   cm.
    Includes bibliographical references
    ISBN 0-86709-365-X (pbk.)
        1. English language—Study and teaching—United States—
Curricula.   2. Education—United States—Biographical methods.
3. Communication in education—United States   I. Title
LB1576.S7988   1995   95-403
375.428—dc20   CIP

Editor: Peter Stillman
Cover design: Jenny Jensen Greenleaf
Cover art: Based on a photo by Cora Lee Five

Printed in the United States of America on acid-free paper
98 97 96 95   DA   1 2 3 4 5 6

For
Alma Patricia Struyk Lambert,

my finest teacher

Contents

Acknowledgments

This essay, like all others, is the work of many individuals. And I am thankful to them.

For the important lessons they taught me about teaching and learning, I thank my colleagues, Jane Denton, Sharon Floyd, and Jay Robinson. While this essay represents my understanding of work that Jane, Sharon, Jay, and I did together with two groups of twelfth-grade students during the 1987–1988 academic year, that understanding is so deeply informed, so much the product of the conversations we had with one another, that whatever is valuable in it must be understood as ours.

For the serious intellectual work they accomplished when they accepted their teachers' invitation to study their lived experiences and literature they were reading and writing in the light of one another, forty-seven twelfth-graders who were my students and teachers during the 1987–1988 academic year deserve thanks. I thank especially Wendy Gunlock, Martha Lozano, Gilberto Sanchez, and Tawnya Voltz for allowing me to reproduce their writing here.

Thanks also to my dear friends who offered generative criticism to developing drafts of this book: Amanda Brown, Cathy Fleischer, David Franke, Cynthia Haythe, Charlie Howell, Laura Julier, Debbie Kinder, Carol Lipson, Jay Ludwig, Michael Michell, Louise Phelps, Faith Plvan, Jay Robinson, David Schaafsma, Janet Swenson, Richard Thomas, Sharon Thomas, and Jim Zebroski.

For encouragement, patience, and good advice, I thank Peter Stillman.

For himself, I thank Bob Boynton.

For all the acts of kindness, love, and encouragement that make it possible for a mother to write a book, I thank Heidi and Andrew: "I lucky to you."

Foreword

This is a book about a journey and a quest. Students and their teachers engage in deepening dialogues with one another, as they work to thematize their own experiences and find forms of articulation for them. It all begins in academic discussion at an English Coalition conference and culminates in a course entitled "Inquiry and Expression," intended to help diverse young people learn to read and to write more effectively. Patricia Stock is one among many who has become interested in narrative as a mode of sense-making; but her study becomes more adventurous and, in many ways, more moving than standard books on qualitative research, on teacher research, and even on storytelling. This may be, in part, because of her beginnings with the work of Mikhail Bakhtin and Paulo Freire, both of whom have opened new doors to a comprehension of the meaning of dialogue and of critical literacy when it comes to opening up the lived world.

Dr. Stock is clearly a participant in an ongoing conversation with regard to language, rhetoric, reading, and writing. She is able to address herself to the existential concerns of students and her fellow teachers without losing touch with her discipline or with the norms that govern it. At once, she demonstrates a most generous sympathy with modes of articulation that are initially defensive, careless, or thoughtless. She knows that many students today, like the ones she taught in Saginaw, Michigan, feel alienated from the ways of expressing themselves characteristic of dominant groups in our society. On one level, no one was particularly interested in initiating them into the dominant rhetoric or style. On another, they frequently suffered from extreme doubt that their experiences were *worth* articulating. It is not unusual, we all know, for a youngster who feels herself ignored or despised or "invisible" to doubt the uses of craft or writing skill. Dr. Stock and her colleagues present a number of stories in which young people are enabled to move beyond such doubt and to choose themselves as living beings whose lives deserve attending to and, at the same time, sharing with others.

There are, indeed, two concepts of "others" in this text. One has to do with the stranger who looks from without and appears to be hopelessly distant, unable to understand. The second has to do with an "other" created in the very act of writing or composition, someone who provides a slightly new perspective and a vantage point for the self-reflection that is always part of the process of learning to say—to write, to read. There is no hint of catharsis in the "inquiry and expression" texts in use in Dr. Stock's classes. The literary texts function to clarify, to impassion, to provide hints and cues as to writing and making oneself clear.

There are relatively brief case histories and writing segments throughout the book, but the centerpiece is "Wendy Gunlock's Intellectual Project." Her teachers, after first assigning generalized themes having to do with growing up, decide to offer her the opportunity to write about her major life concerns. Her teacher-readers also offered her an implied promise that, by interpreting what she was saying, they would enable her to write more communicatively and to say authentically what she herself yearned to say. Patricia Stock offers her readers fifteen or more examples of Wendy's essays, which become more detailed, more shapely, more thoughtful, more perceptive as time goes on. In the course of her writing, she reads various books whose themes somehow connect with hers. Often, she can adopt techniques used by a writer to make a story more interesting and to render it distinctively part of a genre. Wendy, like her schoolmates, writes book reviews as well, gradually opening herself to a sense of intertextuality and a continually widening fabric of meaning.

Dr. Stock surely discovered, as have many of her colleagues, the differences in the lives people live—and, very often, the gulfs that open between our students' lived experiences and our own. Sometimes in these days, we are able to do what Dr. Stock did and offer an essay or a story that tells about our own strivings and difficulties. Sometimes, the tragedies and the losses are so much greater in the lives of children than they ever were in ours that we have (like Patricia Stock and those who worked with her) to develop a particular mode of sensitivity that may serve us better in our efforts to set our students free. There are people today who are asking for a "dialogue across the differences"; and this book may well open up new channels for that dialogue. Surely, few people have used the writing process in precisely this way or attuned themselves in such a way that young people could actually discover the fundamental themes of their lives.

We know from John Dewey and many others the significance of connecting with a learner's actual experience if that learner is to pose worthwhile problems and reach somehow beyond. This book makes it clear that we can find and elaborate on some of the most important themes conceivable as they structure, color, and often fragment young lives. Moreover, it makes clear that the young can create dialogues by means of their texts, dialogues among one another that lead to visions of greater coherence, richer composition, sometimes even transcendence.

The book ends with an approach to teacher research as storytelling: a challenge to objectivism and abstractness in educational research, an affirmation that teacher research is far more than "merely anecdotal." The questions may remain open, as indeed they should; but the dialogue will be all the richer and more meaningful as more and more readers lend their lives to Patricia Stock's writing and discover what story can do.

Maxine Greene
Teachers College
Columbia University

The Dialogic Curriculum

Introduction
A Fresh View of the Field

We must be dedicated to the improvement of schooling. The improvement of schooling is bound to be experimental: it cannot be dogmatic. The experiment depends on the exercise of the art of teaching and improves that art. The substantive content of the arts of teaching and learning is curriculum.

Stenhouse, 1985, 69

What does all this mean for education? One implication has to do with subject matter, with curriculum. Students must be enabled, at whatever stages they find themselves to be, to encounter curriculum as possibility. By that I mean curriculum ought to provide a series of occasions for individuals to articulate the themes of their existence and to reflect on those themes until they know themselves to be in the world and can name what has been up to then obscure.

Greene, 1978, 18–19

During the summer of 1987, sixty elementary, secondary, and college teachers of the English language arts gathered at Wye Plantation in rural Maryland "to chart directions for the study of English in the twenty-first century."[1] Discussion led them to name goals like the following ones for the teaching of English: (1) to make critical literacy possible for all students, (2) to enable students to use language to articulate their own points of view, and (3) to encourage students to respect different points of view. It also led them to identify situations and issues that our profession must consider if we are to accomplish such goals. In doing so, members of the elementary strand drew attention to the structure and lifestyles of families, as well as the media and technologies that surround us. Members of the secondary strand—in a series of composite portraits—dramatized the variety of perspectives and experiences that students in our multicultural society bring to school. Members of the college strand reminded the group of the importance of engaging students as active and interactive learners in courses that use theory and research to focus not only on the uses of language but also on the value-laden nature of those uses. Before their discussion ended, members of the English Coalition

1

concluded that if the goals they named were to be accomplished in schools in our society, our profession would need to develop "a fresh view of the field."[2]

During the summer of 1987, another group of English teachers with similar goals in mind gathered in an elementary school turned into a Staff Development Center during a time of declining enrollments in Saginaw, Michigan. This group, made up of teacher-researchers from the Public Schools of the City of Saginaw and The University of Michigan, was completing a year and a half of work to design, conduct, and study an assessment of the writing competencies of tenth-grade students in the Saginaw schools. I was among them. As the members of the English Coalition were meeting in Maryland to discuss the future of English studies, we teacher-researcher-assessors were meeting in Saginaw to study the writing of students whom—in our assessment—we had failed. (And, yes, the pun is intended.) Looking for common features in students' writing that we might identify and address with instruction, we found something else instead.

The papers our failing students had written were composed of common thematic materials of violence and oppression, and sometimes even of hopelessness and despair. Perhaps we should not have been surprised. After all, taking our students' advice we had asked them to write for four days on the theme of "teenage stress." But the issues and events that our unsuccessful students' inscribed in their writing were more than stressful; in too many cases, they were fearsome. Still somehow, under examination conditions, these students sat in schoolrooms and wrote compositions about those issues and events, and what they wrote moved their readers.

I left our meetings each afternoon with visions from bluebooks swimming in my head, wondering how students had mustered sufficient courage—if not sufficient literacy—to write about the troubling events in their lived lives. Reflecting on the events they described, I could not help but conclude that although students were not ordinarily occupied with writing or talking about these events in school, they certainly must be preoccupied with them when they sat in schoolrooms. I wondered what might happen if one of their courses of study in school invited students to use reading and writing and film and discussion to study the issues that troubled them.

After discussing the idea of such a course in our teacher-research group and securing the approval of authorities in the City of Saginaw Public Schools and The University of Michigan, Jane Denton, Sharon Floyd, and I decided to join together to teach the course to one class of twelfth-grade students in each of the city's two comprehensive high schools. Jane and Sharon are lifelong residents of Saginaw. Reared in middle-class, professional families, graduates themselves of Saginaw's public schools, and respected by their colleagues, their students, and the larger community, both women are intelligent, dedicated educators. At the time, Jane, who is of European-American ancestry, taught in Arthur Hill High School, a predominantly "white" school located on the east side of the Saginaw River in the predominantly "white" section of a city—like many cities in the northeast—with a history of racial tension. Sharon, who is of African-American ancestry, taught in Saginaw High School, an almost exclusively "black" school located on the west side of the river in the almost exclusively "black" section of the city. I, also of European-American ancestry, taught in the Department of English in The University of Michigan and coordinated research projects in the Center for Educational Improvement through Collaboration (CEIC), a unit I helped to establish in the university. Reared in a working-class family in New York City, a graduate of the New York City public schools, I am a living example of a conviction that Jane, Sharon, and I share: Education can provide students opportunities in life that they might not otherwise have.

My colleagues and I were also joined in our effort to develop the experimental course we imagined by Jay Robinson, Professor of English Language and Literature in The University of Michigan. Jay participated in our planning and frequently in our classes so that he might be a fully participating observer of our work.

Inquiry and Expression

Borrowing from Theodore Sizer, we chose the name *Inquiry and Expression*,[3] for the course we hoped might enable students to learn to read and write more effectively, and, in so doing, to gain some useful control over the problems that concerned them. We imagined the course would be realized when students translated a topic of inquiry that teachers offered them in the form of a set of general questions into a number of subtopical studies that were of concern to them and when teachers, in turn, tailored instruction to enable students' inquiries. That is, we imagined that *Inquiry and Expression* would become a course of study when teachers' instructional plans invited students to translate their preoccupations into subjects for disciplined study.

Because we were persuaded that our students would have some possibility to become more effective readers and writers if they read and wrote to inquire into issues that concerned them and that we, their teachers, would have increased possibility of developing effective instructional plans if we joined our students as co-inquirers, Jane, Jay, Sharon, and I planned the *Inquiry and Expression* course around a set of research questions we hoped would be provocative and meaningful to us all. What has been the nature of your growing-up experiences? What are the stories you tell about them? What has been the nature of others' growing-up experiences? What stories do they tell about them? Are there common experiences that characterize growing up and common themes that characterize growing-up stories?

As researching teachers do, the four of us conducted a program of professional inquiry in tandem with the one we conducted with our students. Informally, with each other and with our colleagues in the Saginaw Schools-University of Michigan Collaborative Teacher Research Group, we explored this additional set of questions: How can we teachers plan meaningful, productive lessons for students whose instruction is our responsibility? What is the nature of the teaching and learning that occurs in a curriculum that teachers and students construct in dialogue with each other? And, finally, how can meaningful information about the quality of learning within dialogically constructed curricula be provided to the audiences to whom teachers and students are appropriately accountable: students; teachers, and other professional educators; parents and other members of the local, state, and national communities who have vested interests in students' learning and teachers' work?

Introducing the *Inquiry and Expression* course with a curricular invitation designed to initiate dialogue, we invited students to collect a body of growing-up stories for us to study together. Students collected their own growing-up stories by composing them in the form of free writings and storytelling during our class meetings; and they collected growing-up stories from their parents, grandparents, sisters, brothers, and other members of their communities in tape recordings, field notes, letters, and assorted writings they composed outside the classroom. To the database of these stories, we teachers added our own and those of published American writers whose ethnic heritages matched those of the learners in our classes. Specifically, we read and discussed fiction, poetry, essays, journal and newspaper articles, and films composed and directed by Asian-Americans, African-Americans, European-Americans, Latino/Latina-Americans, and Native-Americans; among them, Ossie Davis, Langston Hughes, Stephen King, Maxine Hong Kingston, Harper Lee, Gloria Naylor, Zibby O'Neal, Rob Reiner, Richard Rodriguez, Leslie Marmon Silko, Steven Spielberg, and Alice Walker.

During this early phase of our work, we also discussed the methods we were using to collect and analyze the narratives we were exploring within our field of study. One way we did this was to compare and contrast the audiotaped interviews that Studs Terkel conducted with individuals from all walks of life across the United States who lived through the depression, transcriptions of those interviews, and Terkel's ultimate inscriptions of them in *Hard Times*. With reference to our own stories, those of published writers, and those Terkel collected, we began discussions that characterized our work throughout the year, discussions of fact and fiction, meaning and value, and the nature and purposes of storytelling.

In the set of questions that introduced the *Inquiry and Expression* course, we outlined a broad field of study within which students might use reading and writing to situate and investigate concerns they faced in and out of school. Individually, in groups, and collectively, students shaded and textured that outline. As they wrote, read about, and discussed their particular concerns, they enriched and extended our understanding of our common concern—growing-up experiences and the stories people tell about them. For example, as one student studied her experiences and the experiences of others like herself who had moved innumerable times during their growing-up years, she not only investigated a personal problem in the stories she shared but also challenged us to consider what effect growing up on-the-move might have on an individual's development. As another student explored his and others' experiences as successful student athletes, his stories invited us to think about the impact on an individual's development of growing up in the limelight.

As a sizable group of students researched their relationships with members of their families, their stories challenged us to imagine ourselves growing up in variously configured modern American families. As another group researched the experience of failing in school, their stories startled us with recognition that unsuccessful students frequently spend most of their time thinking and worrying about school as they are growing up. As several students investigated the function of mischief in their growing-up experience, their stories led us to speculate about when and how responsible adults learn the difference between harmless fun and malicious pranks.

During September and October, as students in the *Inquiry and Expression* course worked to appropriate the questions we posed for study; that is, as they read, wrote about, and discussed their particular concerns in terms of our common one, they not only provided us teachers a wealth of material from which to create literacy and literature lessons, but they also developed a substantial discourse—a rich vocabulary and resonant allusions—to which we could all refer as we taught and learned from each other. For example, on occasions when we wished to speak about the influence of his or her family's traditions on a young person's growing-up experiences, we were likely to say to one another, "Remember Gilbert's mother's story," just as on other occasions when we wished to talk about the conflicts of learning other traditions we were likely to say, "Remember Maxine Hong Kingston's story about learning to talk to her aunt."

From October through January, when students were developing their various research projects and a discourse in which to discuss them, we teachers studied and responded to students' work in consultative fashion. We engaged in what might be called *consultative teaching*, teaching that recognizes the authority and expertise of learners, teaching that encourages learners to identify and articulate researchable issues, teaching that asks researchers to learn necessary information and to develop and exercise competencies they will need to address issues and problems that confront them. As consultative teachers, in individual conferences and in small groups, we discussed the books students were reading, the compositions they were writing, the issues and problems they were identifying and addressing; and we taught students "on the spot" such lessons in literacy and literature as their work suggested they were ready to learn.

During this time when students were developing their various research projects, we customarily began and ended class hours—as students gathered and prepared to leave—with informal talk about different students' developing projects. In this way, students learned about the work of classmates who were not members of the smaller, special interest groups in which they were discussing the books they were reading and the compositions they were writing. Our purpose was to help students weave a web of connections between and among their projects, to help them see how their individual projects interrelated to form our larger one.

In January and February, after they had written and shared many growing-up stories with one another, we asked students to read and compose responses to essays about the adolescent experience written by psychologists, professional educators, and cultural historians who were offering generalizations about the experiences of adolescents they had studied. Specifically, we asked them to read articles written by Mihaly Csikszentmihalyi and Reed Larson, Joshua Meyerowitz, and Theodore Sizer. We planned and taught this part of the course because we wanted students to see how researchers in the human sciences sometimes share the findings of research they conduct into the growing up experience.

As we studied these readings from the human sciences, we met for whole class discussions and invited students to speak to the published authors they were reading from the perspective of fellow researchers. When they did so, we asked if they might be interested in publishing their own research, just as the authors they were reading had published their research. Although the prospect seemed daunting to them at first, our students decided they would like to publish their hard-earned understandings. Accordingly, we designed the last three months of *Inquiry and Expression* to enable students to examine critically the body of literature that they had composed and to select from it pieces that they wished to publish. To do this, students met in groups, reread the compositions that each had written, and recommended to one another selections they thought worthy of further development. Having narrowed the body of literature they might publish, students and teachers surveyed the thematic content of the compositions being considered for publication. After much discussion, students selected a collection of pieces they believed would represent their growing-up experiences in the industrial northeastern United States in the last quarter of the twentieth century. Then, during the last school days of the course and on Saturdays—as their commitments permitted—students from the Hill (Arthur Hill High School) and the High (Saginaw High School) crossed the river that runs through Saginaw to work together with desktop publishing equipment to produce an anthology of their writings, which they entitled *The Bridge: Linking Minds, Growing Up in Saginaw*.

This course of study, that began with a broad set of teacher-developed questions about growing-up experiences and the stories people tell about them and concluded with students' publication of stories they composed to represent their growing-up experiences, proceeded along the lines of several ongoing dialogues that overlapped and intermingled. These several dialogues may be described as of two kinds: *dialogues between self and other* and *dialogues between self and (an)other self*. The *dialogues between self and other* are those in which teachers and students engaged each other; the *dialogues between self and (an)other self* are those in which students engaged with the selves—the personas—they created in the stories they were telling and the literature they were writing.

In the first two chapters of this book, I illustrate these two kinds of dialogues. In chapter one, "The Dialogic Curriculum," as I define and illustrate what I believe to be the distinguishing characteristics of a dialogic curriculum, I dramatize and summarize the kinds of dialogues between self and other that characterized the *Inquiry and Expression* course. In the second chapter, "Wendy Gunlock's Intellectual Project," I reproduce almost all the writing that Wendy Gunlock composed for the course, as well as a detailed discussion of my understanding of the intellectual work her compositions represent. I do this for three reasons: first, to illustrate the substantial intellectual projects that students conducted in the course as they responded to curricular invitations their teachers extended to them and to curricular invitations they extended to themselves; second, to invite readers to form their own interpretations of Wendy's work; and third, to invite readers to judge my judgments of that work.

Because time and space do not permit me to relate all the lessons we teachers of the *Inquiry and Expression* course prepared for our students or the intellectual projects all our students conducted in the course, I have composed the first two chapters of this book—particularly detailed narratives of different kinds—to suggest that which must go undescribed. Detailed as these two portraits are—one focused on dialogues that took place between and among teachers and students, the other on dialogues between students and the protagonist-selves they inscribed in their literature—they do not represent the course of study that we teachers and students constructed together. Such a respresentation would have to account for accrual and interconnection, for all the meanings that learners developed individually and together over time. A course of study is one of those dynamic achievements about which it must be said: "You had to be there." But even if you were—as I was in this case—honesty requires that you acknowledge—as I must—that you do not know the whole story. Much, perhaps most, of the story of the teaching and learning that occurred in the *Inquiry and Expression* course occurred in interactions of which I was not a part. Some of it occurred in dialogues in which I did not participate, some in individual students' thoughts, some of it is happening even as I write.

And so, because I cannot tell the whole story of the course, in the first two chapters of this book, I tell a version of the story, and I claim a meaning for it. I do these things in both the immediate and particular language of narrative and in the distanced and speculative language of theory. Then, in a third chapter, I circle back to the place I began. I reflect on the kind of research my colleagues and I conducted in order to plan and teach and assess our students' learning in the *Inquiry and Expression* course.

Notes

1. Richard Lloyd-Jones and Andrea A. Lunsford, *The English Coalition Conference: Democracy Through Language* (Urbana, IL: NCTE, 1989).

2. Lloyd-Jones and Lunsord, p. xvii.

3. In his important book, *Horace's Compromise* (Boston: Houghton Mifflin, 1984), Theodore Sizer makes a persuasive argument that secondary school English studies in the United States today should be reconceived as studies in inquiry and expression.

1

The Dialogic Curriculum

Language is not a neutral medium that passes freely and easily into the private property of the speaker's [writer's] intentions; it is populated–overpopulated–with the intentions of others. Expropriating it, forcing it to submit to one's own intentions and accents, is a difficult and complicated process.

Bakhtin, 1981, *The Dialogic Imagination*, 294

Through dialogue, the teacher-of-the-students and the students-of-the-teacher cease to exist and a new term emerges: teacher-students with students-teacher. The teacher is no longer merely the one-who-teaches, but one who is himself taught in dialogue with the students, who in turn while being taught also teach. They become jointly responsible for a process in which all grow.

Freire, 1981, *The Pedagogy of the Oppressed*, 67.

Over time, I have come to call the curriculum that we teachers and students constructed together in the *Inquiry and Expression* course, a *dialogic curriculum*. One reason I have done so is because I know that even before I describe what I understand such a curriculum to be, its name will remind readers of discussions about language learning and language use that I was reminded of as I planned for and reflected on the course. For example, I know the name will remind readers of discussions about the nature of language and literature published in the works of Mikhail Bakhtin and discussions about literacy and learning published in the works of Paulo Freire.

In his important book *The Dialogic Imagination*, for example, Bakhtin argues persuasively that the language we use when we talk or write to each other is populated, even overpopulated, with meanings—not only historical meanings accrued during occasions of prior use, but also circumstantial meanings imbedded in occasions of present use. If we gloss the texts we make with our language, Bakhtin tells us, we discover in them multiple voices in dialogue with one another.[1] Or, to put it another way: When we speak and write to one another, we participate–and invite others to participate—in dialogues already underway in our utterances.

In the growing-up stories that students composed in the *Inquiry and Expression* course, I heard the multiple voices, discovered the multiple logics, found the dialogues-already-underway that Bakhtin writes about. For example, in a growing-up story about characters she names Stacey and John, Martha Lozano, an *Inquiry and Expression* student, introduced her teachers and her classmates to the voices and the reasoning of four characters: Stacey; Stacey's mother; John, a boy Stacey "grew up with"; and John's mother. A reader of her writing, I listened to Martha's characters speak through the filter of her understanding. As I did so, I heard the competing patterns of reasoning that shaped her essay and her growing up.

[Growing Up with a Boy Named John][2]

My name is Stacey Oliver. I grew up with a boy named John Stevens. I don't remember being with him as a baby, but our parents have pictures of us together in the same play pen and with the same babysitters. His parents and my parents were very close friends and they spent time together like going to dances, parties, or out to dinner.

I do remember being with him the time we were kids. We played hide and seek, chase, wrestled, and we even played house.

One day my mother and I went over to his grandmother's house to take her an order of Avon she had ordered from my mother. My mother had asked me to take John's mother her order of Avon, since she lived right next door to his grandmother. When I knocked on the front door John came to see who it was. He seen me and he sicked his dog on me. I ran inside the car until my mom came out. I waited for a long time because my mom decided to stay and visit. It was hot in the car but I didn't roll down the window because I was afraid John would unlock the door and let his dog in the car. He stood next to the car door with his dog and told me "Please come out and play," but I didn't.

Growing up with him was fun, while we were kids, but as we became older we didn't talk as much as we used to. We just said "hi" or "bye", and that was it. I think that maybe it was because we reached the age where boys start to like girls and girls start to like boys. We didn't feel very comfortable having a conversation or being together the way we used to be when we were younger. He had his friends and he spent a lot of time with them, just as I spent a lot of time with my friends. I didn't know his likes or dislikes anymore. All of that probably changed when he met his friends. I'd see him once in awhile, but like I mentioned before, we would only say hi or bye.

In June, two of my cousins graduated and my uncle planned a graduation dance for them. There wasn't too many teenagers there, but there were a lot of young adults between the ages of twenty to twenty-eight. I hardly danced with any guys because they were to old so I sat at my table most of the time with my friends. John sat at the table behind me. When I turned around to say hi, he asked me to dance. We danced to a slow song and something about the way he held me made me have certain feelings toward him. I think he felt the same way about me.

About a week later he called me and we talked to each other on the phone for almost three hours. We got to know each other better, the way we used to a long time ago. I felt I had a good friend for life. John called me everyday since that one phone call. We talked about everything, school, clothes, music, people, and even the weather.

When his mom and my mom went to show, my mom said he could come over. That night he asked me to *go with him and I said yes. We shared thought and our feelings, this caused our love for each other to grow more. (* to go with him: to be his girlfriend)

After my parents and his mom found out that we had a special relationship, my mom didn't approve to much because she was very close friends with his parents and if one of us got hurt in a certain way, their friendship would fall apart. My mother wouldn't let me spend time with him because she felt that the more time I spent with him, the more serious our relationship would be. It was to late to worry about that now, John and I were already inlove. I loved him so much that I risked skipping school to be with him. I lied to my mom so that I could be with him, I'd tell her that I was going to be over at a friend's house but instead I would go over to his house. His mom didn't mind if John and I were seeing each other. She liked me a lot because she knew me since I was a baby. Before our relationship she would tell John, "I wish you would talk to Stacey instead of those other girls," she was happy that John and I were together. His mom would cover up for us when my mother called her to see if I was over there or if John was going to meet me somewhere.

All the time we were alone together he wanted to go all the way but he never pressured me. I didn't want to lose him and I thought he might lose his patience if I kept saying no, so one night I said yes and this made our relationship stronger.

A few months passed before I finally knew I was pregnant. No one knew except for John and me, we didn't want to tell my mom yet. She never asked me any questions, she would just say, "You better lose weight because you're getting fat." I think she already knew I was pregnant but she was probably waiting for me to mention it to her. One day I finally did mention it to her and she was extremely upset because John's mom knew before she did. Because of all this, they were now enemies.

I had a baby girl on March twenty-first, it was on a Saturday. All of my family and John's family visited me in the hospital but no one from my family said anything to anyone in his family. John was happy because of our new baby but four days after she was born John was arrested for armed robbery. I didn't want to talk to any other guys or find another boyfriend because I was going to wait for John to get out. He was sentenced to a year and a half in prison. All of my feelings changed during the time he was in there. We don't write letters to each other anymore. I met another guy and I don't want anything to do with John anymore.

Writing about events in Stacey's life—her renewed friendship with her childhood playmate John, her developing involvement with him, her pregnancy, the birth of her baby, John's imprisonment, and her estrangement from him—Martha inscribes various logics that have circumscribed her growing up. In paragraph seven of her essay, for example, she reveals how each of the characters in her story thinks about Stacey's renewed relationship with John. She records Stacey's mother's logic in this way:

> After my parents and his mom found out that we had a special relationship, my mom didn't approve to much because she was very close friends with his parents and if one of us got hurt in a certain way, their friendship would fall apart. My mother wouldn't let me spend time with him because she felt that the more time I spent with him, the more serious our relationship would be.

John's mother's logic, this way:

> His mom didn't mind if John and I were seeing each other. She liked me a lot because she knew me since I was a baby. Before our relationship she would tell John, "I wish you would talk to Stacey instead of those other girls," she was happy that John and I were together. His mom would cover up for us when my mother called her to see if I was over there or if John was going to meet me somewhere.

John's logic, this way:

> All the time we were alone together he wanted to go all the way but he never pressured me.

And Stacey's logic, this way:

> It was to late to worry about that now, John and I were already inlove. I loved him so much that I risked skipping school to be with him. I lied to my mom so that I could be with him, I'd tell her that I was going to be over at a friend's house but instead I would go over to his house. After my parents and his mom found out that we had a special relationship, my mom didn't approve to much because she was very close friends with his parents and if one of us got hurt in a certain way, their friendship would fall apart. My mother wouldn't let me spend time with him because she felt that the more time I spent with him, the more serious our relationship would be.

The characters in Martha's story think differently from one another about Stacey's relationship with John. Stacey's mother reasons that if Stacey becomes involved with John, the relationship will jeopardize their families' friendship; therefore, she tells Stacey not to see John. John's mother reasons that if John develops a relationship with a "nice girl" like Stacey, he will conclude his involvement with other girls whom she does not like; therefore, John's mother encourages Stacey to deceive her mother by visiting with John in John's home. Stacey, assuming that John's interest and attention to her are evidence of his love for her, reasons that "love" justifies her actions and insures her future. John, whose logic we are left to infer in Martha's essay, apparently reasons that telling Stacey he loves her is both the means and the end to the relationship he wishes to have with her.

When Martha wrote "Growing Up with a Boy Named John" for the *Inquiry and Expression* course, she introduced the dialogue already underway in it into the dialogue that was just beginning in our course. When other students and we teachers also wrote stories and introduced the dialogues underway in them into our course, and when we introduced the stories of published writers—rich with the dialogues underway in them—into the course, the voices and patterns of reasoning speaking in our classrooms multiplied. The conversations that developed between and among those voices and those logics proved to be as complex as members of the English Coalition predicted they would be when they told us that the goals they named for teaching the English language arts in our time would be reached only if we learned to understand and account for the variety of perspectives and experiences that students in our multicultural society bring to school.

As teachers of the *Inquiry and Expression* course—in the spirit of the coalition's goals—we took as our challenge not the task of homogenizing our students' understandings, but the task of enriching and extending them. To do so, we invited students in the course to become inquirers, to become more than hunters and gatherers of factual bits and pieces. We asked students to examine the stories they were reading, writing, and discussing by exercising the logic they brought to their school work from their home communities.

That individuals reared in different communities consider different patterns of reasoning logically persuasive is a truism that I need not belabor here. Moviegoers who have seen the 1987 film *Moonstruck* need only recall their amusement watching the daughter in an Italian-American family in New York City convince her father that he should pay for a church wedding and a wedding reception for her second marriage because her first marriage had ended in "bad luck." The daughter reasons that the "bad luck" of her first marriage (her husband was hit by a bus and killed) was caused by the fact that she and her husband were married in a city hall not in a church ceremony, followed by an appropriate reception. While her logic escapes moviegoers, it convinces her father, producing viewers' amusement at the mismatch between their own reasoning and that of the characters in the Norman Jewison film.

Mindful that those of us in the the *Inquiry and Expression* course were not beginning our work together with common understandings of the texts we were reading and writing, we teachers and students concerned ourselves not just with the stories we were studying but also with how we were making sense of them. In the discourse that developed out of our exchanges and inter-actions, we took care to explain to one another how we were making sense of this literature we were reading and writing in order that we might identify and develop patterns of reasoning that allowed us to make sense together–to make common sense.

In classrooms like ours in which dialogic curricula are undertaken, class-rooms in which teaching and learning are conceived as reciprocally realized, reciprocally dependent activities, what counts as logical is not presumed—as members of the English Coalition warn us it should not be—but is constructed of the experiences, the images, the language, the traditions, the values, and the motives of the particular teachers and students who are working to understand a subject at a particular time in a particular place.

Working to examine growing-up stories, growing-up experiences, and the multiple voices and patterns of reasoning that have shaped them, in the *Inquiry and Expression* course we operated within what Paulo Freire calls the dialogic of a "problem-posing" conception of education rather than the monologic of a "banking" conception of education.[3] In practice we composed and read and discussed growing-up stories, and students identified in these stories issues and events and concerns associated with their own growing up that they wished to research in order to understand better both their experiences and how those experiences had been shaped into stories by them and by others.

By grounding their work in issues, circumstances, and events that per-plexed or intrigued them, we teachers planned for students to learn to speak and listen and read and write more effectively by speaking and listening and reading and writing to learn about what concerned them in their lived lives; and we hoped that as students used reading, writing, and discussion to research issues of concern to them, they might also develop deeper understandings and perhaps even greater control over circumstances and events that led them too often to feel out of control.

Let me illustrate how this worked by referring to Martha Lozano's writ-ing once again. When Martha identified issues that concerned her in "Grow-ing Up with a Boy Named John," we teachers and her classmates encouraged her to use reading, writing, and discussion to problematize and investigate those issues. This encouragement came in a variety of forms. One form origi-nated with Martha's classmates. In her writing group, for example, some stu-dents—reasoning along the lines of one or another of the characters in her story—offered Martha advice on how to revise her essay by elaborating and advancing particular characters' reasoning. Other students applauded Martha's invocation of the powerful unspoken reasoning at work in their lives, the fa-miliar, allusive reasoning that made her text as meaningful to them as E. D. Hirsch claims familiar allusions make canonical texts meaningful to classi-cally educated readers.[4] For example, after reading the passage in Martha's story that understates John's reasoning, Elexandria remarked: "I've heard that line before, and I know where it ends up."

Following her classmates' responses to her writing, we teachers also encouraged Martha to probe issues she had raised in "Growing Up with a Boy Named John." Responding to the story from our own perspectives, perspectives informed by our own patterns of reasoning, we asked Martha if she would be interested in exploring the reasoning of the various characters in her story by writing a series of follow-up stories in which she featured the perspective and experiences of one or another of those characters. When Martha indicated she was interested in doing that, we posed questions about the reasoning of the various characters in her story that we thought she might be interested in investigating. With respect to Stacey's mother's reasoning, we asked, for example: Does Stacey's mother disapprove of Stacey's involvement with John just because the families' friendship might be jeopardized by it? Has she left unspoken other objections she might have to the relationship? If so, what might they be? With respect to John's mother's reasoning, we asked, for example: What are John's mother's concerns for her son? What are her concerns for Stacey? With respect to John's reasoning, we asked, for example: What does John say or do to indicate that he is concerned for Stacey's well-being? For the well-being of the child that is going to be born to Stacey and him? As John sees it, what are his responsibilities to Stacey? To their unborn child? How does he plan to realize those responsibilities? With respect to Stacey's reasoning, we asked, for example: What will life be like for Stacey when she is pregnant? When she is a mother? Who will care for Stacey and John's baby? And what will caring for the baby mean to the characters in Martha's story—Stacey? John? Stacey's mother? John's mother? the baby?

Our teacherly questions took the shape of curricular invitations to Martha. In Freire's terms, we did not offer Martha bankable solutions to the problems she implicitly posed in her writing; rather, we offered her questions to investigate. During the year of the *Inquiry and Expression* course, in her storytelling, Martha pursued these questions and others. For example, in a growing-up story she wrote after "Growing Up with a Boy Named John," Martha explored the quality of life of an unmarried teenage girl. Following advice from her writing group and in response to questions raised by her teachers, as she played out the reasoning of a character like Stacey in "Growing Up with a Boy Named John," she also dramatized the life of an unmarried teenage girl.

[Alone on a Friday Night]

I was in love with my boyfriend, Joe, and we always talked on the phone and spent time together. I loved him so much and I would do anything for him. I was already pregnant and I loved him even more.

One Friday night I called him and his mom answered the telephone. I said, "Hi, is Joe home?", and she told me "No, he's not here right now, he left with Raul, but he should be back by 11:00 pm." When I heard her say that he had left with Raul, my heart started beating fast and I was thinking to myself that they were both out with other girls, I felt mad and hurt at the same time and I wanted to break up with him.

After 11:00 pm I called him back but he still wasn't home and I felt like beating up someone. I knew I couldn't take it out on my sister or any other family member, so I let some of my anger out by crying. I kept calling every ten minutes but he still wasn't home. I knew his mother was getting mad because I kept calling and it was already 2:30 am. She told me she would have him call me when he got in, but I was so mad that I kept calling anyway.

Finally, I got dressed and started walking to his house to wait for him. It was 3:30 am and I was already walking down the street alone in the dark, pregnant. I didn't think of what could of happened to me, like getting raped, getting chased by a dog or even getting killed, all that was on my mind was what time Joe would be home, where he was, and what girl he was with.

When I was almost at his house I thought about how stupid I would look waiting for him on his front porch. While I was walking I did a lot of thinking. I thought about trusting him. I felt that if I really loved him, I should trust him, and we would have all day Saturday to talk about it. I thought of the danger I could of put myself and my baby in by taking my anger out on walking over there and waiting for him. I felt better when I walked. I think that the walk calmed me down and cooled me off because I felt hot inside from being so mad. The walk also made me feel better so I just went back home and fell asleep.

The next day we talked and I wasn't mad anymore. If he would of called while I was mad we would of probably had a fight and broke up and I would of been going through more stress.

Told from the perspective of an unmarried, pregnant teenager, "Alone on a Friday Night," records poignantly a bright young woman's ambivalent and erratic thinking as she works to make logical sense of the situation in which she finds herself. At home alone one Friday evening, uncertain of where her "boyfriend" is and with whom, the narrator in Martha's story describes the emotional stress she experiences. Although she distrusts her boyfriend ("When I heard her say that he [Joe] had left with Raul, my heart started beating fast and I was thinking to myself that they were both out with other girls."), she feels guily for doing so ("I felt that if I really loved him, I should trust him. . . ."). Although she is angry with her boyfriend ("I felt mad and hurt at the same time and I wanted to break up with him."), she is afraid to be so ("I thought of the danger I could of put msyelf and my baby in by taking my anger out on walking over there and waiting for him"; "If he would of called while I was mad we would of probably had a fight and broke up and I would of been going through more stress.").

The mother who cautioned and warned her daughter to avoid a relationship with the boy she grew up with in "Growing Up with a Boy Named John" is absent from "Alone on a Friday Night" so is the boyfriend, whose name is Joe in this story. In "Alone on a Friday Night," Joe's mother is not pleased with her son's girlfriend as John's mother was in Martha's earlier story. In fact, she is "getting mad" because her son's pregnant girlfriend is calling her home every ten minutes between 11:00 p.m. and 2:30 a.m. on the Friday night that Martha writes about.

Left with the consequences of actions that others participated in, the pregnant teenager in "Alone on a Friday Night" is a character Martha, who is also an unmarried, teenage mother, can relate to. She is a character Martha can write about and with, can talk to and about. In textual form, she is a character with whom Martha can sympathize, about whom Martha can be critical. She is a character Martha can imagine and reimagine.

If the first reason I have named the kind of curriculum we developed in the *Inquiry and Expression* course a dialogic curriculum is to invoke the work of theorists of language and literature and literacy and learning like Bakhtin and Freire, a second reason is to evoke the work of contemporary philosophers of education and curriculum theorists who acknowledge their indebtedness to John Dewey. Arguing for the salutary effects of conceiving curriculum as inquiry and students as inquirers, these scholars believe that students' spoken and written language is their most readily available, most powerful means of learning.

For example, Maxine Greene, the preeminent philosopher of education in the United States today, argues for such a conception of curriculum in her important book *Landscapes of Learning*. In Greene's view, the lived world must be understood as the structuring context for sense-making of any kind, even for scientific inquiry. Because she considers learning to be "a process of discovery and recovery in response to worthwhile questions rising out of conscious life in concrete situations" (19), Greene believes that curriculum should provide students opportunities to reflect on the predicaments of their lived world in the context of the studies they are asked to undertake in school. She puts it this way:

> Students must be enabled, at whatever stages they find themselves to be, to encounter curriculum as possibility. By that I mean curriculum ought to provide a series of occasions for individuals to articulate the themes of their existence and to reflect on those themes until they know themselves to be in the world and can name what has been up to then obscure.[5]

Because we teachers of the *Inquiry and Expression* course share Greene's understanding, we invited our students to create a curriculum with us by articulating the themes of their existence and by using reading, writing, and discussion to reflect on those themes. Students took advantage of our invitation, and over the course of the year, we watched them identify the places and roles they occupied in the world. We watched them name what might perhaps have previously been obscure to them. For example, even as Martha Lozano wrote a series of growing-up stories about unmarried, teenage women, she also wrote about her experiences as a teenage mother, living in her parents' home with her young son. In compositions like "Living at Home," an informal piece of writing she composed in twenty minutes during a class session, Martha reflected on her situation in the world in such a way as to suggest that she was using her writing to clarify some of the predicaments of her lived world. In "Living at Home," Martha also appeared to be using writing to clarify the predicaments of others with whom she lives.

[Living at Home]

There are days when I just can't stand it anymore. I usually have arguments with my mom about my son, there are times when he wants to play with his toys and my mom complains because she wants to get her rest. I get so mad that I feel like hitting her, but she's my mom and I can't hit her so I'll cry to let out my anger. I feel that I have to kill myself sometimes because of this but the reason I am still existing on this earth is because I have friends who care, a son who needs me, and a God that loves me. I know my mom and I should get along well, but it's really hard because I have a baby of my own and she just had another baby. There's not enough room in the house for all of us to live there, but the only reason I haven't moved out is because my mom takes care of my son while I'm in school and she wants me to graduate. If I move out, I'll flunk in school because it will be hard for me to be on my own with my son and go to school, if I stay at home, I'll have more arguments with my mother about my son. I feel that I don't have enough freedom for me and my son in my mom's house, we're limited to certain things like, when he can play, what time I should do my homework and when we can sleep. It's pretty hard at home and I go through a lot of stress. I really feel like killing myself, but I know I have a lot to live for and a lot to offer this world and my son.

Teachers whose students choose to explore in their classrooms themes like those Martha Lozano writes about also hope, as Greene does, that when students name the worlds in which they live they take a promising first step toward making and remaking those worlds beneficial for themselves and others. With Greene, my colleagues and I believe that the kind of schooling, the kind of curriculum, we worked to construct in the *Inquiry and Expression* course for Martha and her classmates holds some promise of leading students to what Greene calls *praxis*, "a kind of knowing that surpasses and transforms, that makes a difference in reality."[6]

In addition to philosophers of education, like Maxine Greene, whose work influenced ours in the *Inquiry and Expression* course, is a host of curriculum theorists of the English language arts—among them, Nancie Atwell, David Bartholomae, Ken and Yetta Goodman, Dixie Goswami, Shirley Brice Heath, Ken Macrorie, Anthony Petrosky, and Eliot Wigginton—to name just a few working in the United States today. These teacher/researcher/theorists have developed model inquiry-based curricula and have demonstrated their benefits for students in elementary, secondary, and college level classrooms; in cities, suburbs, and rural areas; from Maine to Florida, from California to the Carolinas. One whose work also influenced Martha Lozano is Shirley Brice Heath. Martha learned about Heath's work through a letter exchange with me.

Shortly after the *Inquiry and Expression* course began, a number of students asked me why I was so interested in reading and writing. In response to their questions, I wrote students a letter that told them something about my growing-up experiences:

Dear Students,

I became a serious student in my seventh and eighth grades in school. I realize that now. I also realize that I became a *practiced* reader and writer during those two years as well. Furthermore, I believe the two phenomena are related.

At the time I was becoming a serious student and a *practiced* reader and writer, I was a lonely and insecure thirteen- and fourteen-year-old. I was lonely and insecure, in part, because I was a young teenager, but only in part because I was caught between childhood and adulthood. I was lonely also because I was a bit of an outsider in my community. I lived in a Hungarian-American community, and I wasn't Hungarian-American. But my ethnic difference from my schoolmates wasn't the whole reason for my loneliness either. I lived in a small, rural community with few children, and we were separated from one another by distances too great for children to travel alone. Finally, I didn't have many interests in common with my classmates. The boys seemed interested in the cutest girl. And that was not I. The girls seemed interested in the boys and the girl the boys were interested in. The long and the short of it are that I had time on my hands.

I took to books. I checked out all the books I was allowed from the travelling bookmobile that visited my school once a week; I read them in a day or two and then counted the days until the bookmobile would come again.

In the books I read, I found worlds in which I could live and participate. Because my own world was unsatisfactory, I loved the world of books. I read enough to become a *practiced* reader.

The story of how I became a *practiced* writer is related, on the one hand, to my habit of reading and, on the other hand, to how I became a serious student.

When I was in seventh and eighth grades, I attended a first-through-eighth-grade elementary school at the southern tip of Staten Island, one of New York City's five boroughs. Public School #4 was a one-room schoolhouse with rolling walls that slid opened and closed on slick tracks. When the rolling walls were opened, all the school's students could be in one room for assemblies or announcements or special programs. When the walls were closed, students in first and second grades studied with a teacher in one room; in third and fourth, with another teacher in another room; fifth and sixth, with another teacher in another room; and seventh and eighth with still another teacher in still another room.

As a result of the fact of the physical arrangement of students in classrooms and the fact that there were usually only fourteen or fifteen students at each grade-level each year, teachers at P. S. #4 had a real challenge in helping their students to learn. In my seventh- and eighth-grade classroom, for example, Mr. Romano had twenty-eight pupils, fourteen seventh graders and fourteen eighth graders. He taught us English, history, science, mathematics, art, music—whatever he knew.

As I reflect on that time now in an era of departmentalized junior-high-school instruction and specialty teachers, I marvel at what Mr. Romano accomplished. He asked his pupils to help one another, to teach one another.

He made each of us believe we were expert at something—at the subject he observed we liked or handled successfully.

Because I liked to read, he asked me to read to others, to help others with reading. I did; and as I did, I learned how to think about reading, how to think about others, how to think about learning. I didn't know it then, but I do realize now that I began to think about learning then.

Mr. Romano made me a writer. He did it kindly when he might have embarrassed me instead. Because I got bored at times in our class of students with varied interests and abilities, sometimes when Mr. Romano was presenting a lesson, I would open a book in my lap, under my desk, and I would read. One day he stopped at my desk when we students were working at some assigned task. He set down a speckled, hard-covered composition book and said, "Those books you read in your lap . . . write about them in here."

I did.

I came to be a good reader because I practiced reading. I came to be a good writer because I practiced writing. Because I read and wrote effectively, I did well in school. Reading and writing have had the most direct impact on my school learning that I can identify.

Sincerely,
Patti Stock

In response to my letter, Martha composed the following message to me:

I liked this story a lot because I learned something from it. What I learned in this story I will tell my little boy when he's old enough to understand. You become good with practice. Your story was interesting, where you lived when you were young, how the classroom system was. Your school teacher, Mr. Romano sounds like a caring teacher. I care a lot about my son, and I want him to have caring teachers.

This story has taught me that there are ways to spend your extra time wisely. You spent your's reading and writing and now, you know what you are talking about when you come to our class to talk about writing.

To a teacher who was trying to teach by offering students opportunities to translate the preoccupations of their lived worlds into intellectual occupations in their school world, who was asking students to bring their lived experiences into productive dialogue with their school work, who was trying to teach, not by correcting students' sometimes infelicitous uses of spoken and written language, but by modeling forms of spoken and written language that would serve them in school, Martha's message to me was gratifying. Responding to it, I gave Martha a copy of an essay Heath wrote with an unmarried, teenage mother, Charlene Thomas.[7] Based on field notes Thomas kept to document times when she read to her infant son and audiotape recordings she made of her son's experiments with spoken language, the essay is a substantial study. On a Post-it, I stuck to the essay, I wrote, simply to Martha:

Martha, thanks for your kind note. Since you are so interested in your son's learning, I thought you might enjoy reading this essay about another mother who was interested in her son's learning. P.S.

In response, Martha wrote:

October 23, 1987

Dear Dr. Stock,

Thank you for the packet on "The Achievement of Preschool Literacy for Mother and Child." It contained some interesting information such as reading with your child while he's in preschool or even before he starts.

The other day I recorded him. I was saying 'ba" (bottle) and he was calling me "Da Da." He also did alot of gerbering and made sounds. I think I'll save that tape.

. . .

Sincerely,
Martha Lozano

P.S. I'm working hard on my stories.

Martha's letter to me reveals that she learned one of the lessons I hoped to teach her and her classmates when I wrote to them about becoming a practiced reader and writer: Martha's letter is dated, and contains a standardly formed greeting and closing. I did not correct the first message that Martha wrote me to include these customarily expected features of friendly letters, yet she adopted them. She learned them in the way that all of us learn the forms of spoken language: by engaging in purposeful dialogue with others. My dialogic response—composed in the form of a friendly letter—to questions students asked me taught Martha the formal features of such letters without my having to tell her what she had been too often told in school—that she didn't know how to write. The fact is, Martha did know how to write, and she knew how to think critically about complex material. Anyone who has read the case study composed by Heath and Thomas knows it is an essay, written to and appreciated by an audience of professional educators. Apparently, because it spoke to an intellectual project Martha had named and was pursuing—How may an unmarried, teenage mother be a good teacher for her son?—the essay was not too demanding for her to read, understand, and use. Martha never mentioned to me that she had any difficulty reading it, although she frequently talked to me about mentioned parts of the essay she found interesting and useful to her.

Students, like Martha, in the *Inquiry and Expression* course, and like those in the Basic Reading and Writing Course in the University of Pittsburgh that David Barthomomae and Anthony Petrosky write about in *Facts, Artifacts, and Counterfacts*, seemed able to position themselves in a field of study that held some familiar landmarks. They also seemed able to move from the positions they originally occupied in that field toward others by engaging in disciplined studies that made sense to them—and that they made sense of—as they travelled the course of their study.[8] For example, moving from her initial interest in the experiences of unmarried, pregnant teenagers, experiences with which she was personally familiar, Martha Lozano used the occasion of the *Inquiry and Expression* course to explore in concrete specificity issues of broader concern in her lived world and ours, among them, the nature and quality of relationships that young men and women in our society are establishing with one another today, the impact of alcohol and drugs on the lives of young people in the United States, and the widespread violence in our society. In a story she chose to include in *The Bridge*, Martha demonstrates not only an understanding of issues that concerned her, but also a literary style she developed during the course of her study.

In the Wrong Place at the Wrong Time

Robert, also known as Bob, my mother, and I sat at the kitchen table one Friday afternoon, when we got into a conversation about funerals.

As we were eating the oatmeal raisin cookies my grandmother used to make before she passed away, Bob said, "She used to bake real good cookies. I wish she were still alive."

As if she were still there at the funeral, which had taken place five years before, my mother remarked, "Remember all the people who showed up at her funeral? I wonder who's going to be at my funeral?"

"You don't have to worry about me," Bob assured her. "I'll be at your funeral, and if I die first, you have to promise you'll be at my funeral."

"Sure I'll be there," my mom answered, "but that's not how it will be, thank God." Then the conversation ended, and Bob left to get ready to go out.

That night, Bob and a few of his friends were getting together at a girl's apartment. It was sort of a party. Only a few people were going to be there, but there was going to be drinking and smoking. Bob was looking forward to being there.

During the afternoon, Bob was at his cousin's house getting ready for the party. He was showering, ironing his clothes, and combing his hair.

A close friend of Bob's, Anna was cleaning her upstairs apartment, knowing that people would probably stop in to visit since it was Friday night. She talked to her sister and a couple of friends on the phone, and they all decided to go over to her apartment to drink. Anna's small party was growing.

Bob, too, had talked to some of his friends to see what they were going to do that night, and they also talked to Anna and decided to go over there. The small party had grown.

As he prepared for that night, Bob kept thinking of the things he used to do for fun as a little boy, like watch cartoons, play with his toy cars with the little boy next door, and imagine he was a king. But now that he had grown, his childhood games and fantasies had given way to a different kind of fun. Although he couldn't understand why, he thought about his family and relatives. He couldn't get them out of his mind.

Anna's sister's boyfriend, Mark, and another friend of theirs were already at the apartment. They were sitting around talking quietly and getting high until the rest of their friends came.

Bob and his friends Mike and Frank were driving around in Mike's car just to waste a little bit of time before they arrived at Anna's because they felt it was still too early to arrive.

Bob was in the front seat, lost in his thoughts about his past, how he loved his family, how he failed in school and then dropped out, how he wished he could change his life. He knew drinking was wrong and that sometimes it could get him in a lot of trouble, but he was used to it, since he started drinking at an early age.

Anna and her friends were in her apartment laughing and telling familiar stories as they waited for Bob, Mike and Frank. On their way to the apartment, they were supposed to stop at one of those stores that lets anybody buy liquor. They wanted to buy more liquor themselves.

While Anna and her friends were in the apartment, a strange man tried breaking in because he thought no one was home. The door had been unlocked, so he just walked in, and when he saw that they were drinking, he didn't want to leave.

Mark stood up and yelled, "Get the hell out of this apartment before I kill your ass!

The man refused to leave so Mark kicked him down the stairs.

Meanwhile Mike made his stop at the store and purchased the liquor. Bob and Frank waited in the car. While he waited, Bob wondered to himself. He wondered if he ought to be hanging around with these kinds of people. After Mike bought the liquor, they were on their way to the apartment.

Back at the apartment, the intruder became extremely angry because he had gotten kicked down the stairs and an argument started between him and Mark. Mark threw the stranger out into the yard and pulled out a knife and stabbed him.

Bob and Mike could see the struggle because they were only one block away. The car reached the curb in front of the apartment and Bob stepped out of the car to see what was wrong. In one quick movement, the man pulled out a gun and shot Bob straight in his heart. Bob died instantly with his eyes open, looking as if he was still thinking about his family, his friends, and his life.

During the year we worked together, Martha Lozano used the occasion of the *Inquiry and Expression* course to investigate issues she associated with her growing up, issues of significant concern to her. Almost always she did so with an end in view: She wanted to understand how she might rear her son so that his growing up experiences would be healthy and happy and ones that would lead him into a healthy and happy adulthood. Throughout the school year, Martha appeared to strive for "a kind of knowing that surpasses and transforms, that makes a difference in reality." Whether she used her reading and writing to learn how to teach her son to read and write or to confront the horror of the violence that surrounds her and us, Martha developed and exercised a purposeful literacy as she placed the voices and patterns of reasoning in her home community in dialogue with those she met in school.

The third and final reason I have chosen the name dialogic for the curriculum I illustrate in this book is because I hope the name will become emblematic of the book's argument: Unless and until students appropriate their teachers' instructional plans and translate those plans in their own terms, into their own intellectual projects, even the best-laid plans of teachers or curriculum developers remain just that—plans. If students are not able to relate what they already know to what they must come to know and to become full participants in courses of disciplined study that enable them to think new and different thoughts, to develop new and different competencies, for all intents and purposes, they are disfranchised from learning. Curriculum in school is realized dialogically by active learners, or it isn't realized at all.

The Distinguishing Characteristics of a Dialogic Curriculum

Conceived amid the thought and work of theorists and practitioners who have argued the benefits of inquiry-based curricula, a dialogic curriculum has its family resemblances. It also has its distinguishing characteristics. When asked to describe what I understand those characteristics to be, I mention four.

- A dialogic curriculum is introduced when teachers invite and enable students to join them in a broadly outlined field of inquiry.

- A dialogic curriculum is established when students ground the curriculum in topical inquiries—issues, questions, problems—that their prior experiences have prepared them to explore within that field.

- A dialogic curriculum develops as learners enable one another to enrich and extend the understandings and to improve the competencies with which they entered the field on inquiry.

- A dialogic curriculum concludes when learners carry their enriched and extended understandings and their improved competencies back from their inquiries into their home communities.

Outlining a Field of Inquiry

When they outline the dimensions of a field of inquiry with a set of broadly conceived questions, teachers define the territory within which a dialogic curriculum may be constructed. Teachers design these broad topical questions to serve three constitutive purposes: first, to enable them to teach both the content and conduct of their disciplines, interdisciplines, or subject areas; second, to enable students to be active learners and to make sense of their schoolwork in terms of the images, language, and logic they bring to it from their prior experience; and third, to enable students to enrich and extend their understandings of a subject as they study it in school and to improve their competencies to continue to conduct studies of that subject after they leave school.

In the *Inquiry and Expression* course, for example, the questions that defined our field of study—What have been your growing-up experiences? What are the stories you tell about them? What have been other people's growing-up experiences? What stories do they tell about? Are there common experiences that characterize growing up and common themes that characterize growing-up stories?—served these purposes. First, they enabled us secondary school English teachers opportunities to introduce and engage our students in literacy and literary studies in the reading, writing, and discussion of imaginative literature, literary criticism, sociology, and social criticism. Second, they invited students to collect and compose growing-up experiences and understandings that enabled them to address the study at hand—to enter into the inquiry. And third, they enabled students to enrich and extend their knowledge of literature and experience and to improve their ability to use the English language arts in the service of their self and communal expression.

It is generally understood today that learning requires would-be learners to engage actively with the subject matter they would learn. Whether or not students are invited and enabled to be active learners in school has much to do with the manner in which the subjects they are to study are introduced to them. If we teachers of the *Inquiry and Expression* course had introduced our twelfth-grade students in public schools in an economically depressed city in the northeastern United States to the work of our course with a statement like this one: "Our subject in this course will be 'Growing up'—The Story of the American Experience as Presented in Imaginative Literature," rather than with the set of topical questions we posed, we would have positioned them differently than we did in relation to the subject we wanted them to study. We would have positioned them as consumers of prepackaged knowledge rather than as the collectors, creators, and critics of knowledge that we wished them to become. By introducing our course of study in literature and literacy with a set of topical questions, we positioned students as active participants, as co-composers of the curriculum. We said in effect: "We are all able to contribute to this study, and we are all able to learn from this study. We will all teach one another, we will all learn from one another, and we will turn to other experts and authorities to teach us."

When students began their work in the *Inquiry and Expression* course by composing their own growing-up stories, they wrote themselves and their histories into the study. When we grounded the lessons we wished to teach in the stories our students composed, we invited them to become active learners in our study, and we did something else as well: We indicated that the lessons we would teach depended on their being so.

Grounding the Inquiry

Once begun, a dialogic curriculum proceeds when students identify aspects of their lived and textual experience in which they are able initially to ground the inquiry their teacher has outlined. For example, when students in the *Inquiry and Expression* course collected and composed stories about aspects of growing up that interested them, they became inquirers in corners of our field of study that were at least somewhat familiar to them. As they identified subtopical studies that their prior experiences had prepared them to investigate, they named themes, issues, problems, and questions they were positioned to study purposefully and productively.

For example, when Gilbert Sanchez introduced the following growing-up story he collected from his mother into our course of study, and when he told us that the story was about learning how to work and earn a living, he named a subtopic of our larger one that he was prepared to invest himself in studying.

> We, as a family, the Sanchez, come from a generation of working on the fields. Now, we . . . we learned how to work on the fields by our grandparents. They thought us had to work. And, as we growed up, we learned how to work on the sugar beets, and we used to come from Texas to Michigan, and then we worked for six months, and then went back to Texas. So this kept going on until we were grown up. And then, as we got married, we thought our kids had to work on the . . . on the fields. But, our reason was to show them how to earn their money because working on the field is hard work. And I used to tell my kids, they have to learn how to work, so they can buy their own clothes for school. Which . . . we could afford it, but the main point was for them to learn how to earn their money. And they had to work hard, because I had that experience as I grown up. And this is how our generation, from our parents came, and we passed it to our kids. So, all my three boys, they learned how to work on the fields, and how hard it was to earn their own money.

Responding proactively to Gilbert's contribution to our emerging curriculum, we teachers helped him translate an issue of concern to him in his lived life into one that could occupy him and his classmates in literacy and literature studies. Because Jane, Jay, Sharon, and I were planning the *Inquiry and Expression* together, we not only thought about how we might translate the materials that our students were introducing into our classes into productive instructional activities, but we also talked about how to do so. The discussions we had about Gilbert's mother's growing-up story and our class' response to it illustrate my point.

I invite you to return with me to a warm September afternoon in Saginaw and to watch us teachers discuss what happened the day when Gilbert introduced the audiotape of the story his mother told him into the *Inquiry and Expression* course. I invite you to listen in on us that day and on a subsequent one when Jane, Jay, Sharon, and I planned to use the story as the basis for several literacy lessons we wished to teach our students. I ask you to join me in my remembrance of these occasions, because I want to make it clear that teachers who plan for and teach dialogic curricula are not unusual teachers doing unusual things. On the contrary, we are teachers who do what most teachers do: We think about our teaching and our students' learning, and we discuss our teaching and our students' learning informally in dialogue with one another. What may distinguish teachers of dialogic curricula is that we base instruction in our classrooms on the lessons we learn from thinking about and discussing with colleagues the ordinary, everyday occurrences in our classrooms. Curriculum and instruction in our classrooms are not only integrally related to one another but also to the ways in which our students translate the curricular invitations we present in instructional activities into their own intellectual projects.

So, return with me, please, to the classroom students have just left as Jane and I begin to reflect on Gilbert's mother's growing-up story in preparation for our work to build lessons based upon it.[9]

I closed the door behind the last student to leave the room. Jane unearthed her contraband Winstons and the seared tuna fish can that collected their tell-tale ashes and headed toward the window. She lit up, drew in, and exhaled, "Do you believe Gilbert's mother? Now, that is some lady."

Eager to relive the moment, I paced around as I let Jane's train of thought ride and embarked on one of my own, "Could anything have been better? The kids were incredible."

"I didn't know what to expect when he offered to go first." Jane rolled her eyes.

"Me either. I thought: Okay, that's it. He's probably collected a story from a long-lost uncle who's been at sea for twenty years. It will be remembered for containing more four-letter words than any story ever told—certainly any ever told in a school room." I could see Gilbert's face. "He was smiling, Jane. Smirking. You know. As if . . ."

"No, no. He wasn't smirking. He was nervous."

"Jane! Gilbert? Nervous? Give me a break. He's a con artist from the word go."

Jane and I deconstructed the teaching-learning moment we had witnessed until Gail Oliver and Bea Ugartechea joined us a few minutes later. Happy for the audience that required we retell the incident from the beginning, we told our colleagues what had happened in our fifth-hour class:

I began, "Today the kids were due to begin sharing the growing up stories they collected from family members—older family members."

"Mmm," Bea signaled me to go on. "Guess who—you will never guess who—offered to go first."

"Who?" Bea asked, not exactly from the edge of her chair.

Jane took over, "Gilbert Sanchez."

"Gilbert?" Bea smiled quizzically, tipping her head to one side, knowing there was more to this story.

Jane repeated herself, "Gilbert" as I began to describe her efforts to get the room of more than thirty restless twelfth graders to turn their attention to the task we were about to take up a half-hour before lunch.

"I asked the kids to take out the growing-up stories they collected from the older members of their families and for someone to volunteer to go first."

Gail interrupted, "Did they have stuff?"

I nodded. "I was surprised. When Jane asked them to take out their stuff, there was a lot of paper shuffling. And I could see that some of them had tapes."

Jane confirmed my observation, "I didn't see an empty desk. Honestly. So, anyway, I asked them again, 'Who's going to go first?' Then, Gilbert raised his hand."

Bea broke in, "Well, that's it."

"What's what?" I asked.

"He just popped a tape in a tape recorder, told someone to tell a story, and he was done. No muss, no fuss, no bother."

I nodded, "That's what I thought too."

Jane interrupted, "But wait. You haven't heard it yet."

Gail encouraged Jane to resume the story, "Okay, so go on."

Working to recreate the atmosphere in the class, and no doubt trying to add to the suspense, we placed students in the room, particularly our most notorious students, and we described what they were doing when Gilbert raised his hand. Like Gilbert, our class had a reputation: Almost all of our students were biding their time until high school was over for them; some were in danger of not graduating at the end of this or any other year. Because Bea and Gail had at one time or another been the teachers of most of our students, they enjoyed imagining the scene in the classroom with us.

I continued, "When he started the tape, Gilbert's mother's voice was soft. It was hard to hear her. The kids started to quiet down. I rewound the tape. This time when it began they were quiet; they were really curious, I think."

"What was the story she told?" Gail asked.

Jane summarized Gilbert's mother's words, "She told about growing up in Texas and working on the fields and coming to Michigan and trying to teach her children how to work hard in the fields, not because they needed the money, but because they needed to learn the value of earning a living."

I interrupted Jane, "The thing is . . . It was the sound of her voice. It was gentle, melodic. You had the sense that she was telling Gilbert something important. You know . . . in a way, she seemed to be addressing an audience beyond Gilbert. Maybe she was imagining the class . . . Gilbert playing the tape for the class. You know? Her voice was mesmerizing. When the tape ended, nobody said a word. No one spoke. You could have heard a pin drop."

"What did Gilbert do?" Bea asked.

"He just sat there."

"I didn't want to be the first to say something," I said.

"No, I didn't either," Jane added. "I wanted one of the kids to say something. There was a long pause, and then John said, 'That's the kind of story my mother tells, too.'"

I interrupted, "Jane pushed it. She asked: 'What kind of story do you mean?' And then slowly, still very quietly, the kids started to talk, saying things like: 'You know, about how hard they worked.' 'About the kinds of things we don't appreciate.' 'About the bad old days.'"

Jane elaborated, "The kids started to ask Gilbert things. You know like:

'Where were you born?' 'Were you born in Texas or here?' 'Did you ever work in the fields?' 'Where?' They started to talk among themselves. Gilbert was the center of the conversation but not entirely. Somebody said, 'I was born in Missouri. My father was in the army.' Then kids started to ask each other where they were born, and a lot of splinter conversations developed."

"I heard somebody ask someone who he had collected his story from. Somebody else asked, 'Did you do a tape?'"

"Meanwhile, the whole time, Gilbert was talking. Sometimes to a couple of kids; sometimes to the whole class. He became the discussion leader, sort of."

"And, another thing. He wasn't showing off. He was just being natural. I don't think I'd ever seen him engage in natural, comfortable conversation before, now that I think about it. He's always playing a kind of game in class."

"When things started to quiet down, Jane said something like, 'Before, John said, 'My mother tells that kind of story, too.' I want to come back to that. Your mother doesn't tell a story about coming from Texas to Michigan to work in the fields, does she, John? You are not a Sanchez?'"

"The kids liked that, there was a fair amount of speculation about the likelihood of John and Gilbert's being brothers."

"The kids took it back to learning more about Gilbert though. Someone else asked him if he ever worked in the fields."

"Remember, Martha intervened there with, 'I thought you worked at Little Caesar's?'"

"Yes, that set off another round of talk about jobs the kids had."

"We stayed out of it. We didn't try to bring it back to the genre issue. I tell you I learned a lot listening to them. Gilbert was born in Michigan, and he has worked on the fields, harvesting sugar beets . . . ."

"Anyway, I thought they were generating a lot of stuff we could go back to. And they surely were breaking the ice for taking up some issues later."

Gail interrupted, "What do you do with him though? He didn't write anything. Where do you go with it?"

"Well, he did the assignment," I responded first. "That was a breakthrough with Gilbert. And '*the story*,'" Jane punctuated the air with quotation marks, "was a real opening for us."

"How so?"

"Well, for one thing, it gives us a chance to talk about the kind of a story *that kind of story* is, you know. We can get into form, genre, right away now by getting them to talk about what kind of a story this was, how it's going be the same and different from some of the other stories we'll get. And it was a showcase of the values that have shaped Gilbert's growing up-experiences."

I came in, "I'll tell the world. In a lot of the informal talk that I could hear the kids were identifying themes that are sure to be important in growing-up stories and how they get shaped: work—their parent's, theirs, their parent's pressure on them to think about work after school; relationships—to their parents, to themselves. . . . There was a lot of that."

Jane reinforced her earlier observation and went on, "And the notion of conventional stories is in the air, you know, stories parents tell to shape kids' values. . . . You know what got to me was the way they talked together and then in pairs and then together again. It was as if someone were orchestrating it. It happened sort of gracefully. They were spinning a web and then venturing out on it. They were meeting themselves coming and going. Lots of connections were being made: 'I come from there too.' 'I worked in the fields once. It's too hot.' 'You should work at Little Caesar's.' 'I work at McDonald's.' 'Where, on Holland?' 'My mom's on me to get a job all the time. She's always telling me that she had to take care of the little kids at home, and she doesn't want that for me. She wants me out in the world, working.'"

A student knocked at the door and postponed further discussion of Gilbert's mother's growing-up story and our class' reaction to it until several days later. During a weekly planning meeting, Jane and I told Jay and Sharon about Gilbert's mother's growing-up story to explore how we might use it as a vehicle for teaching in our course.

Jane introduced the subject, "We were so lucky this week. Gilbert Sanchez offered to share the growing-up story he collected from his mother. He played an audiotape of an interview with her. I don't know if we've mentioned him before, but Gilbert is an absolutely no-school-work kid. Smart, but lazy. So when he offered to be the first to share a story, I was really surprised. When I saw that his story was audiotaped, I thought he was taking the easy way out of the assignment. And, he probably was."

I interrupted Jane to pose one of the questions implicit in our recollection of the moment: "I wonder, Jane, do you think he was surprised by the reaction to his mother's story, or do you think he went first because he knew he had something special in the story? Something of his own that was going to work in school?"

"Now, that's an interesting question," Jane commented to me and then turned to Sharon and Jay to give them more background information about Gilbert. "You know, Bea knows a little bit about Gilbert's family. His older brother was a serious student, and there is support for education in the family. But Gilbert has always played around in school. He stays just this side of flunking out of school."

"So what was the story?" Sharon asked.

I picked up, "In a mesmerizingly gentle voice, Gilbert's mother told about how the family had come to Michigan from Texas to work in the fields. She explained that she wanted her sons to work in the fields, not for the money the way she had but because she wanted them to know the value of hard work. She wanted them to know what it means to have to work hard to earn your way. She began to speak by saying something like: 'We, as a family, the Sanchez . . . we come . . . .' It was a wonderful opening. The kids didn't expect it; we didn't expect it, not an opener like that. You know, now as I'm repeating it again, it makes me think we can take up story openers, like: 'Once upon a time . . . ,' 'You don't know about me without you have read a story by Mr. Mark Twain . . . ,' 'In the beginning . . . ," that kind of thing, and how those openers work to signal genres. Gilbert's mother's story was a kind of abstract parable."

As Jane and I told Jay and Sharon about Gilbert's mother's story, the four of us began to analyze it from our perspective as teachers of the *Inquiry and Expression* course. Jane raised her hands and marked her words with quotation marks drawn in the air, "The issue of 'kinds of stories' was raised by one of the kids. John opened it up when he said something like, 'My mother tells 'that story,' too. He put his finger on the concept of genre, and we are going to be able to use that for sure."

I continued, "After Gilbert played the tape, the kids asked him questions, and he asked them questions, and they started to talk about where they had grown up, where their parents had grown up, what their parents did for a living, what work they wanted to do. A lot of background information was being shared, and the kids seemed comfortable with it. More important, now that I think about it, they were asking each other questions. The talk was inquiry oriented: They were posing questions that they or someone else might take up. That's it: They are posing research questions."

Jane intervened, "No, not really. They were just asking for information."

"That too, Jane, but I think I'm right. That was there, but so was something else. I'm thinking about questions like Martha's as she was trying to get at the similarity in their experiences as Chicano/Chicana children: 'Do you think all Chicano kids are told to work hard like that? I was always made to watch the kids at home.'"

Sharon added her analysis and criticism when she raised the issue Bea had posed, "He didn't write anything? He just played the tape?"

Jane answered, "Right. I think we've got to do something about that. We've got to give some kind of assignment to the kids who didn't write their stories in one form or another."

Sharon agreed.

"We could transcribe the tape and . . . How long is it?" Jay asked.

"Not long," Jane answered with interest. "What do you have in mind?"

"We could transcribe it as one long sentence and ask the kids to translate the spoken text into a punctuated, written one. They could play around with the syntax and paragraphing and then compare the versions they develop," Jay explained. "That would give them a chance to work with it, to linger over the language. They'd be studying Gilbert's mother's story and working on the punctuation of the written language at the same time."

Sharon was pleased, "I like that . . . linger over the language."

"I really like it because I'm worried that we're not doing anything with grammar or mechanics with the writing we've been getting," Jane remarked.

"And we can use it in both classes. That will give them something in common," Sharon added.

"You know," I continued, "this paves the way for the Studs Terkel stuff we thought we might use. You know, the tapes of the people he interviewed for *Hard Times*, and the transcriptions of them, and the pieces that actually appeared in the book. That would be a great way to get at the similarities and differences between speaking and writing."

"And, maybe we can get into language variation issues, too," Jay suggested, offering to look around the bookshelves in his study for activities that invited kids to try their hands at dialectology.[10]

Sharon sealed our plans just as our favorite waiter at Holly's arrived with our lunch, "I like it. Let's do it."

And we did.

In the fashion I have just reconstructed, we teachers of the *Inquiry and Expression* course studied our students' responses to our curricular invitations and developed literacy and literature lessons based on them. One of the literature lessons we developed later in the semester, as it happens, was also based on Gilbert's mother's growing-up story. It had become clear to us that a number of students were preoccupied with the theme of work so we initiated a study of theme by asking students to read an excerpt from Richard Rodriguez' *Hunger of Memory* in the light of Gilbert's mother's story. During a class discussion of Rodriguez' experience working with other Mexican-American laborers one summer when he was in college, students related Rodriguez' account of his work experience to Gilbert's mother's account of working in the fields and to Gilbert's discussion of his mother's account. Students questioned Rodriguez' interpretations of his experience, just as they had questioned Gilbert's mother's and Gilbert's interpretations of their experiences. They compared and contrasted the experiences, trying to put themselves in Rodriguez' place, Gilbert's mother's place, Gilbert's place, their own places. They examined the ways in which Rodriguez' version of his story and Gilbert's mother's version of her story had been shaped into texts in Rodriguez' book, in Gilbert's tape, in our transcriptions of Gilbert's tape, our class discussions of Rodriguez' and Gilbert's mother's story, and so on. And, I would argue, students read Rodriguez critically because Gilbert's story had positioned them to do so. The experiences and stories that Gilbert had shared with his classmates not only invested him in their study of both Rodriguez' experience and his narrative composition of it, but they also interested Gilbert's classmates in that study.

Co-composing the Curriculum

In the fashion that I have described, teachers of dialogic curricula offer curricular invitations to their students and base goal-oriented instruction in the materials and ideas that students introduce into their classes in response to those invitations. That is, planning for and instruction in dialogic curricula take shape in teachers' proactive responses to students' contributions to the curriculum. In their responsive lesson planning and consultative teaching, teachers not only receive and acknowledge students' contributions to the curriculum, but also shape additional curricular invitations for both individual students and the classroom community.

Again, I use Gilbert's work to illustrate my point. In the *Inquiry and Expression* course, when Gilbert told us that—like the first audiotaped story he contributed to our curriculum—others he wrote were also about work—about his work at Little Caesar's that was hard and frustrating; about the illegal work of thieves; about his fears that there would be no work for him after school—he identified an interest that promised to draw him into school work. We not only were able to guide Gilbert to undertake a personal program of reading and writing based on these initial contributions he made to our course, but also were able to help him discover in them other themes and issues for study.

We began to expand the topical studies Gilbert would investigate in the *Inquiry and Expression* course when he introduced this second story into the curriculum, a story he composed in writing, a story that clearly begins where his mother's story left off:

> My mom keeps telling me I need a job, Im gonna go out and some application. So I applied at Little Cersars Pizza. I knew a friend their and he told me he could get me in, he was my girlfriends brother and also my friend, we grew up together playing football in the neighborhood, he was a couple of years older than me, but anyways within a week they called me and told me I started work the following wednesday. I was so excited and happy. My first job. Well not really because my mom would take me to the fields and I would earn my money their. It was kind of traditional for our family to work their, my parents had to work their for a living for a while but now it was different we would go so they could teach us how to work and how hard it was and so we would know how to earn our own money. I called my girl-friend which lived out of town in Holland, Michigan. She use to live down the street from me. I could just run down there and give her a little kiss, now I have to save my money and drive down there and visit for a couple of days. I called her and told her that I got a job, she was happy for me. I started thinking about how it would interfer with my friends because we like to hand out. They told me, the first day of work, if we was going out, I told them I had to work, but they understood. Working their at the pizza place is alright but I don't plan on staying their long. One friday I asked for it off and the manager said ok. So me and my boys went out to a football game, we was all walkin like we was "Bad", just chillin and this guy comes up to me and said are you Rubens brother. I told him "yeah whats it to you" now this guy thought he was bad, he thought he could kick my ass right, excuse my language and he had all his friends with him and I had all my friends with me and me and my boys are real close, its like we all brothers, we blood and blood thicker than water know what Im sayin. so I told the guy "Well I dont like you" and I cocked my fist back and hit him straight in the face, but before that happened while he was talkin I reached in my coat pocket and grabed a lock and then thats when I hit him Im pretty sure I busted his nose he went down for the count and his guy tried to hit me. I kinda moved out of the way and my boy Ken hit him with a right, Pete hit him with his left and Monty "takes" came in and blasted him in the face and he was threw. There was a big fight cause we didn't stop we kicked ass that night. We got a couple of blows from them to. cause I remember going home in pain, my

ribs was kinda bruised. I told my girl what happened when I went to see her
in next week, she was a little upset, not that I fought, but because I could of
gotten hurt, she love me, and I love her. Her parents let me visit her, meaning they let me stay right there, her parents are wonderful people. I still think
theirs a lot more adventure to get into cause Im still growing up. When Im
alone in my room, sometime I stare at the wall and I say to myself I goes
"self, life is hard but it gets harder you know, life is just beginning. Whats
gonna happen if your girl goes to a different college out of state, then you go
to, whats gonna happen if you dont get a good enough job for you to support
your wife, you know what, you have a lot of pressure on your back." just
sittin there—chicken. My parent been gettin on me becasue I haven't been
going to church in a long time. Part of it is because of work, the other part is
I dont want to go. I have my reasons why, you wouldn't understand or maybe
might. I don't really like having a conversation about the Lord because I feel
like a hypocrite cause here I am talking about him and I don't even go to
church. When you walk with the Lord, it isn't easy cause sometime you fall
down, and the Lord picks you up, and when you fall you have to try to get
up. Know what Im sayin. I fell pretty hard. Its been a longtime. lately Ive
been thinking of my future, its scary sometimes.

After Gilbert shared this story in class, we asked him a simple question:
"What is the story about?" When he told us it was about work, we mentioned
to him several other things we thought it was about also (violence, boy-girl
relationships, loyalty, gangs), and we suggested he ask several of his classmates what they thought the story was about. Specifically, we suggested that
Gilbert ask his classmates to read his story, to bracket sections of it that they
found interesting, and to name in a word or two the growing-up themes (topics, issues, problems, concerns) that they thought Gilbert was writing about in
those sections. In so doing, we made an essential move of teachers in a dialogic curriculum: Teachers in a dialogic curriculum ask students to pose curricular invitations for themselves and one another and to use the resources
available to them to learn what they need and want to know. That is, teachers
in a dialogic curriculum teach students to become self-directed learners.

In response to the help he asked of them, Gilbert's classmates told him
that they thought his second story was about many things: boyfriends and girl
friends, uncertainty about the future, racial tension in Saginaw, bad jobs, to
name a few. In fact, they thought that Gilbert's essay was about too many
things "at once." They advised him to write a story about each of the themes.
After his classmates' reading of his story, Gilbert reread it and told us that he
thought it was also about his temper and his love for Tina.

In the third story he wrote, Gilbert decided to take up the curricular invitation his classmates offered him. He decided to write a growing-up story about
one of the themes imbedded in his second story. The theme he chose to explore
was one he had identified during his rereading of the story—his temper.

One time me and my friend Pete was in class and the teacher was talkin,
teaching class. Pete was talking and the teacher that it was me. he said "Gil-

bert down to the office "I said "for what" in a real nice tone of voice and the teacher was being smart he goes "You know for what and quit acting dum" so I got upset I said "Dont talk to me like that Pete my best friend tried to calm me down and Pete told the teacher he said "Gilbert wasn't even talking and he told Pete "shut up or you can go with him Pete told him he said "Man your a ——————" the teacher just said "Get out of here" I told him "shut the ———— up" the teacher said somethin I can't remember. I said "————— you". I lost my temper. I went to the office well we went to the office and the Principle asked us what happened and we told him what happened and we told the truth but then he heard the teacher side of the story and he wasn't telling the truth, he was lyin in front of us. We didnt say anything, Me and Pete just looked at each other and said "man he lyin". So we got suspended I told my Pops everything that happened My Dad told me "you should go apologize for loosing your temper "he was right I shouldin of lost my temper. I waited a couple of weeks before I apologized but my Dad didnt tell me go apologize He just suggest that I do. if he would of told me too I wouldn't have done it. and that what happened.

When Gilbert read his story in class, many of his classmates, who, like Gilbert, were at risk of not graduating from high school, responded to it by reciting injustices they had experienced in school. Hearing in their stories less reflection than we wished, I composed a growing up-story in which I tried to place an injustice I had experienced in school in perspective. I shared the story with students the next day. In doing so, I made another move that characterizes responsive teaching in dialogic curricula. I took advantage of students' interest in a topic at hand to teach a lesson in literature and literacy by offering them a model of a story that reflected on itself, not a model beyond their reach, but one they might approximate.

Unfairness

Genie and I had arranged that I would copy her notes in study hall. I was still coughing and tired from the flu that had kept me home from school a week, but I was trying hard to catch up on the work I had missed in school.

Study hall was quiet. Mrs. Gordon was a tyrant. We sat in straight, close lines and did our work until Mrs. Gordon felt like chatting, that is, until she finished her work. Then she started conversations with her favorites. Genevieve Morelli, my friend, who sat in front of me, was one of her favorites.

When we settled in, I tapped Genie on the back. She passed me the geometry notes. I began copying, hoping to get through the whole week's worth of proofs in that hour. I wrote and wrote, little aware of the others in the room. When I looked up, Mrs. Gordon was staring at me accusingly. I tried to smile at her, uncertain of why she was looking at me as she was.

She asked with a taunt in her voice, "Busy?"

I nodded.

"Cheating?"

I was almost wordless, "No."

"Yes, you are."

"No, I'm not. I'm copying Genie's notes."

Genie intervened, "She is, Mrs. Gordon. She's copying my geometry notes. She was absent."

From behind her pearl-rimmed glasses, Florence Gordon's eyes said, "A likely story." She said nothing.

She always treated me as if I had cheated. It was unfair.

Some time later, when Mrs. Wright saw Bill Hicks cheating on the geometry regents' exam, we were all amazed. Not only had she seen him from an unlikely place (she was in a third-floor room on a courtyard kitty-corner from the room in which he was swapping papers with another student), but Bill would also lose all his regents' credits. We had all been warned in the formal instructions before every regents' exam we took. Maybe he'd never go to college, we speculated in little cliques in the hall when we learned the amazing news.

But, in fact, Bill did not lose his regents' credits. He just did not get credit for the geometry exam, and he went to college, University of Vermont, as I recall. We thought the school made an exception because his father was an important man in the community. We didn't think it was fair.

After college, I heard about Bill again. His name came up many years later in a conversation with a high school friend. Mrs. Gordon and Genie and Mrs. Wright's images were playing in my mind when Diane Scrafton—who lives in Hawaii now— told me that Bill was one of the first Air Force pilots to fly in Vietnam. He was the first New Yorker to be killed there.

More and more, I wonder: What's fair?

Students attended carefully to my story. To be sure, they were interested in the fact that I, a teacher, had been treated unjustly in school. But they were more interested in the untimely, violent death of my high school classmate. It gave them pause. After a time, they began to talk of uncles and cousins and fathers who had been in Vietnam. Talk of war, death, and injury at an early age displaced stories of school injustices.

The next story Gilbert wrote takes shape, I would claim, as a response to the one I read in class. It also takes shape as an intertextual installment in the text Gilbert was composing about his growing up experiences, a text that began with his mother's story; a text that went on to introduce his job at Little Caesar's; "his brothers" and his loyalty to them; his girlfriend Tina and his love for her; his troubles at school and his friend Pete; a text that now begins to anticipate an adult world to which his youthful one might lead. Like his earlier stories, the one Gilbert composed in response to my story about injustice may be read as both a dialogic contribution to the discussion that developed about injustice in our class and to his investigation of the issues of personal concern to him.

As I grabe a hold of the iron bars with the cold, dark cell at my back, I look out into the bitter morning, my last day of being locked up in my own world with so little freedom. I cant help but to feel sad when joy should cover the pain I suffered in my heart. the thirty-five years of being seperated from society has come to the end. I have a fresh beginning on life, but I cant ever forget what we once had.

It started from the time when we were all just learning to know what life is about. we were very close friends Brothers is what we use to say we were and we treated each other that way. We were all so similar but yet so different.

Ken came from a rich family, Rich boy, everything came to him so easy. Lazy bumm. Everything came so easy for him, parents handed him everthing he needed. wanted, dreamed of. Ken wasn't just another spoled rich kid, he was fun loving and very trusting. He always had this rugged look on him. Ken was the biggest and biggest and strongest of the three. He never took anything senior unless it was the business we were all involved in.

Pete came from a broken family and lived with his dad "Pops". Pete was the guy who could talk well with people you know what Im sayin he was the one who could handle people in his own unique way. All the ladies loved him for that and his boyish look in his face. He always held a grug. A grudge against the world.

As for me I carried fear with me everywhere I went. It was just the cold look on my face. I lived on my own in the ghetos staying any where I could mostly with my brothers Pete and Ken accepting their parents as mine. I carried similar trait of both of the guys. I was kinda in the middle of them both. a cross between Pete and Ken I always took everything I did seriously.

We all shared the love we had fore each other, understanding one another. We all shared the love of the same career. Back then we were just Punk low ranksters use to rob banks.

As every day went buy we grew more mature in our work, our little own maffia. Every day we met new people making new connections all over the States. At our early age we surprisingly ran a whole town. We always new where and what each of us were doin. As you know every business has their competition or apponent.

The Herreras ran their own rob squade. We grew up with them, we were always fighting. with them beating up each other. They had power behind their back. but we had the strongest background from our fathers.

It all went down one day We were all at Kens house just the three of use drinking some fortie of colt 45. The three of us decided to do outside and sit on the porch. Ken walked out first. and I was the last. As Ken stepped out the shooting began. the herraras were there waiting destroy our future. Ken stood alone pulled out his 9mm we all had so many shots against the odds of 10 to 1. Pete jumped behind the railing I jumped behind the wall of the open door. Ken stood their firing his pistol hitting as many as we could. I could here the cry of his voice over the loud thunder of guns. I ran out to watch Ken as he fell to the ground. It was just me and Pete, with no hope. Me and Pete looking at each other stood and shot as many as we could. as I fell the floor all I could think about was that is over. I heard the cars pull away I woke up wounded in several places lying next to my closiest friends my brothers both dead. After being hospitilized for several weeks I was tried for murder among other things and was found guilty sentence to thirty-five years of imprisonment.

Now, here on my last few minute in my cell I think of how the would will accept me my family. I think of how cruel the society could be to an ex-convict. I wonder what my life would have been like after.

As Gilbert composed his action-filled fiction, he did so, no doubt, in the forms familiar to him from watching R- and X-rated films and the many hour-long gangster programs that follow half-hour-long sit-coms on television. But his story is also shaped by the life he lived with the "brothers," by the lives lived by his friends and their families. Students in our class—not just Gilbert—had experienced murder in their community, some in their extended families, some in their immediate families. Having come close to death, fearing death, it is perhaps not surprising that Gilbert chose to reflect the possibility of death at an early age in dialogic response to a story his teacher composed about, among other things, death at an early age. Neither is it surprising, perhaps, that Gilbert chose to reflect on the possibility of death at an early age by creating a fictional character who watches his friends being murdered, who murders others, who lives with the consequences of murder, and who wonders what it all means to him and to his family. In a dialogic curriculum, just as teachers teach responsively by using students' contributions to the curriculum as the basis for their lessons, students learn responsively by incorporating teachers' lessons into their understandings and their competencies.

Several weeks after I introduced my "Unfairness" story into Gilbert's class, I introduced it at another appropriate moment into the class that Sharon and I were teaching. In that class, too, students were moved by the death at an early age of my high school classmate. Students' reactions to my story and the growing-up stories that they composed in response to it, stories that explored their experiences ranging from injustices experienced in school and at home to death and violence, led Jane, Jay, Sharon, and me to introduce Stephen King's novella *The Body* and Rob Reiner's film version of King's novella, *Stand by Me*, into our classes. After our reading of *The Body*, we asked students to compare stories they or their classmates had written about the themes of death or violence or physical or verbal abuse with the same issues in Stephen King's story, which our students knew was based on one of his growing-up experiences. Tawnya Voltz used the occasion to compare King's novella with the following growing-up story she composed for Sharon and me early in the school year. In her story, Tawnya raised issues she explored intertextually across the *Inquiry and Expression* course.

> A story that I will tell my child, about my childhood is the time I got a whooping because I didn't know how to count money.
> One day when my mother, my father, my two sisters and I were getting ready to go somewhere. We had our coats on and everything. My mother had given me some change. When she gave it to me she told me how much it was, so I ran up to may father, showed him the change, and told him how much it was. By my father always trying to teach us different things, he told me to count it. I would count the number of coins, then when I get to the last coin, I would say the amount of money I had. he took me in the living room, took the lamp off one of the end tables and spreaded the coins out and kept making me count them. I would start crying, he would make me be quiet, but

he kept making me count the coins. he had everyone to take their coats off. He made me count that money all day until I got it right. We didn't even get to go to where we were getting ready to go. After I got finished counting the money he told me to go lie down. He left, then my mother told me I could get up if I wanted to. I got up and went in the bedroom where she was. I guess she felt sorry for me spending the whole day counting money. It made me feel good.

In comparing her story with *The Body,* Tawnya explored the character and nature of physical force and the intentions that provoke it:

Dear Mrs. Floyd and Dr. Stock,

Both the novella and my story tells of something tragic. The novella tells about a group of kids going to look for a dead body. My story tells about how I was spranked for not knowing how to count money. I feel that the novella was tragic because it is sad to know that someone your age is dead. Knowing that they didn't have a chance to attain their goals in life. My story was tragic, well at least I thought it was, because it didn't feel to good to have something pondered in your head. I knew that I would learn how to count one day, but I guess my father felt that should be the day and he made sure that what he felt became true. The book and my story seemed to be similar in another way because both of them delt with someone older being foreceful or mean to someone younger than they are. My father was being forceful to me in trying to make me count, while in the book, the older guys was mean to the younger ones, because they wanted to claim that they found the boy's body. both the story and the book was something that happened to someone when they were younger and recalling as they remember it. You can actually see what happens because it comes to you as if it happened yesterday. It seems like I can still see my father's face as he kept telling me to start counting the money over, and when I began to cry, he would hit me with the belt, and tell me to be quiet and to start counting. When I looked in his face, he had an angry face, but I knew, well at least, I know now that he meant well.

The novella and my growing up story was similar, yet they had a lot of difference in them. the novella dealt with a dead body, while my story only told of me being spanked. Also, when you think about a person being dead, you know that the law is involved, yet in my story, it only involved my parents and I, although at the time I probably wished that the police would make a house visit. *The Body* also had some amusing parts that story, but even as I look back on my incident, there isn't anything there that I find the least bit amusing. Although each story was tragic, both of them ended smoothly. In each story, I found something that was hard to believe. In the book, I found it hard to believe that a group of young guys can do something to hurt another young guy. In my story, I found it hard to believe that my father would canceled plans, just to sit at home and make me count money. I also would have never beleived that my father would go so low as to spanking me until I count the money correctly. When my father was spanking me and yelling at me, all I could think about was how mean and hateful he was. I wondered why he went through all that on that particular day to make me county money.

As I wrote that story, it made me think about his intentions. I thought about his intentions because I never really had a reason to think about or recall that situation. When I got to thinking about what he did, I began to think that he wanted the best for me. That was a hard way to make me count, but he did it anyway. I feel he could have waited, but it's to late for that now because he has already did it, and I know how to count now. Since I was taught to count money in a forceful way, I will try to be as gentle and patient to my child as I can, but if he began to act like he is not trying, I will try a firmer method.

In Tawnya's letter to Sharon and me, she not only responds to the curricular invitation we have extended to her but also to a curricular invitation she has extended to herself: an invitation to better understand the provocation for and consequences of an event from her childhood that she remembered well. Tawnya continued to work to understand this issue across the *Inquiry and Expression* course. For example, later in the school year when we were reading Alice Walker's book, *The Color Purple*, excerpts from her reading journal reveal Tawnya's continuing efforts to probe the uses of physical force in families:

> I really enjoyed the story. When I read it, I just couldn't figure out why Mr._ treated Celie the way he did. She use to work like a slave. I was also shocked when Celie didn't mind Shug staying with her and Mr._. She didn't mind him sleeping with Shug. Then I realized she didn't mind because that way, she didn't have to worry about Mr._ beating on her. I thought the story was interesting, but I didn't like the way men felt that they had to beat their wives in order for them to behave . . . .
>
> . . .
>
> When reading *The Color Purple*, I got the impression that Mr._ (Albert) was a cruel man. I figured that because he started hitting on Celie almost the first day she was there. He use to talk to her like she was a puppy. He use to go and meet Shug, and make Celie help him get dressed. He moved Shug in their house when she was sick, and he made Celie cook for her. When Shug was staying with him and Celie, he use to sleep with Shug. He also yelled at the children. He tried to tell Harpo not to marry Sofia. As the story went on and he became old and Celie had moved away with Shug, it seemed like he realized he was wrong, when he did all those things. Sofia even told Celie that he had started working in the yard and keeping the house clean. By the end of the story, him and Celie had become good friends. They use to sew together. I feel that the author might have presented him that way at first, to show that everyone is capable of making a change in themselves.
>
> . . .
>
> Nettie was a real smart person. She was capable of taking care of herself and she went to school. Nettie was smart because she never let her father nor Mr._ take her to bed. She ran away or did whatever was necessary to keep them away from her. She use to try to teach Celie how to read, and she use to tell Celie to stop letting Mr._ beat on her. Nettie had never been

pregnant. Nettie stayed with Celie and Mr._ for a while before Mr._ made her leave. When she left, she wrote Celie, but she never recieved her letters. She had almost traveled all over the world. Later in the story, she got married, because of love, not force. At the end, she and her family, meaning her husband and Celie children moved back home where Celie was. At first, Nettie was staying in Africa.

. . .

The book gave me more feeling than the movie. When I read the book, I could feel every emotion the author presented, whether it was excitement, anger, sadness, etc. the author did a lot to show Celie feelings and how her feelings went from sad and afraid to angry and hate. She also made Sophia's attitude and feelings very clear and blunt. I could understand Sophia's feelings in the movie better in the movie than in the book. The movie and the book showed that she wouldn't take any mess off of anyone. I really liked that about her. She even hit the mayor. You could understand Sophia if you watch the movie instead of reading the book.

When Gilbert used the instructional activities to explore and extend his initial concern with the issue of work and Tawnya used them to explore and extend her initial concern with the uses of physical force in families, they did what students in a dialogic curriculum do. To paraphrase Maxine Greene's words: They articulated the themes of their existence and reflected on those themes until they knew themselves to be in the world and until they were able to name what had been up to then obscure.

When Gilbert and Tawnya named themes in their lived worlds that had previously been obscure to them, we teachers encouraged them to investigate those themes and develop complex understandings of them. For example, during the *Inquiry and Expression* course, we not only encouraged Gilbert to explore the subtopical question, What is the nature and place of work in the passage from childhood to adulthood?, but also to investigate a number of other subtopical questions that surfaced in his writing and in class discussions. Among them were these: What are the characteristics of a dutiful son? An exemplary brother? A loving husband? A responsible parent? What does school offer young men who have been prejudged, stereotyped? What are the prospects for such young men, who so often drop out or are unsuccessful in school, to earn living wages? What are the requirements of friendship? When is loyalty to childhood friends appropriate/inappropriate? What is the likelihood that a young man whose friends have found themselves in prison will find himself there? What are the chances that a young man whose friends have been killed will himself be killed? What are the chances that a young man whose friends have killed will himself kill? We not only encouraged Tawnya to explore the subtopical question, What are the reasons for and implications of the uses of physical force in families? but also to investigate a number of other subtopical questions that surfaced in her writing and class discussions. Among those questions are these: How can parents rear their different children consistently and fairly and still meet their different children's different needs? How can a young mother, who also happens to be a talented and hardworking student, successfully juggle the responsibilities of home and school?

A dialogic curriculum develops as students explore the dimensions of their initial interests along thematic lines charted by their emerging and intermingling inquiries. Over time, as teachers draw students' interests into conversations with one another and as students unfold the layers of complexity and interconnection contained in their inquiries, their intellectual projects inevitably overlap and intermingle. In the *Inquiry and Expression* course, for example, as Paulette and Dexter and Brian and John read, wrote, and talked about mischief, they not only found commonalties in their understandings of the topic, but also differences. In class discussions, one of them would say, "I did something just like that," or "No, you've got that wrong, it isn't like that." As they involved one another's inquiries with their own, we advised them to form a special interest group in which they might compare and contrast their experiences, their readings, and their developing understandings of mischief. These students began to describe the similarities and differences between the mischief in which they had engaged and about which they were reading.

They carried the habits of their inquiry into a whole class meeting one day when Jason distinguished the mischief they were exploring from the violence that several students in another special interest group were exploring. Dexter had just told a story about dropping rocks from a highway overpass onto vehicles moving below when Jane asked him what the story was about. Dexter replied with a mischievous smile, "Mischief."

Jason disagreed. He made his case with another story, this one about a young man who dropped a bowling ball from an overpass near Detroit, killing the driver in a car below. "Your story is about violence," he said.

Silence filled the classroom until Jane broke it to pose a curricular invitation that led to a most productive class discussion: "When do childhood pranks stop being childhood pranks? What distinguishes childhood pranks from violent behavior?" In her proactive response, Jane made a move typical in a dialogic curriculum. Based on the relationships that students were beginning to recognize between and among their projects, she framed a broader and more complex issue for their study. In moves like this one, over time, teachers and students in a dialogic curriculum enrich and extend their understandings of the subject of study at hand. Charting conceptual maps, they probe more deeply and more broadly into the intellectual territory they are exploring together.

Perhaps it is also interesting to note here that my original reason for proposing that my colleagues and I develop and teach the *Inquiry and Expression* course was that I wondered what would happen if students, who were frustrated and, in some cases, debilitated by serious problems in their personal lives, had the opportunity to undertake disciplined study of those problems in school. Because my colleagues and I were not persuaded that the violence, oppression, hopelessness, and despair that surfaced in bluebooks of students we had failed in our assessment of tenth graders' writing were preoccupations of all our students, we introduced the *Inquiry and Expression* course around a broader set of topical questions. These questions allowed students who were preoccupied with difficult personal problems to explore them and students who were not to investigate other issues. Nevertheless, difficult personal problems figured significantly in the writing of individual students and special interest groups, and eventually in both our classes.

That was the 1987–1988 academic year. Now, as I enter school buildings with guards at their doors, walk through school hallways where weapons searches are underway, or watch students and teachers scanned with metal detectors, I understand what our students knew then. The symptomatic stories *Inquiry and Expression* students were telling Jane, Jay, Sharon, and me foreshadowed the epidemic with which we live now.

Representing Learning

Toward the end of their work together, teachers in a dialogic curriculum invite students to shape their individual and collective learnings in a form they can carry back into their home communities, not because the larger study is ever exhausted, but because time runs out. Although *The Bridge*, the collection of narrative essays that students composed and published to represent their growing up experiences, demonstrates their learning in the *Inquiry and Expression* course, it should not be understood as synonymous with assessment in the course. The publication of end products of students' course work constitutes only one of the three forms of assessment that are characteristically conducted within a dialogic curriculum. The first two forms of assessment—to shape instruction and to shape learning—are integrally related to the dialogic construction of the course of study itself. The manner in which the first two forms of assessment was conducted in the *Inquiry and Expression* course is illustrated in the first two chapters of this book.

The third form of assessment in a dialogic curriculum, the form that functions to display students' learning to parents and other members of the local, state, and national communities appropriately interested in that learning, has other purposes as well, purposes that are intended (as the first two forms of assessment are) to enrich and extend learning. It enables students to circulate their learning back into their home communities. In so doing, it not only invites students to think about how their school work relates to their lived lives, but also to experience the social consequences of publishing and distributing their ideas.

To fulfill the third form of assessment in the *Inquiry and Expression* course, students worked with their teachers first in small groups, then as whole classes, then as a partnership of two classes, to compose, publish, and distribute a collection of their growing-up narratives. After deciding that their published work should include at least one piece from among the best writing each of them composed, students selected the articles they wished to collect in the anthology and arranged them chronologically. Beginning with the earliest memories they associated with growing up and ending with the most recent ones, they meant to tell a story made of stories, a story about the development of personalities and the construction of potential.

The content of their collection decided, students produced a book. Some used desktop publishing equipment to produce camera-ready copy of its parts. Others copyedited and arranged its parts into a book-length manuscript.[11] With teachers' guidance and advice, students developed flyers, contacted area bookstores, and arranged for a book-signing party for authors; their families; interested citizens in the community; and newspaper, radio, and television reporters.

Composing their work in the form of narrative essays—the kind of literature they had read and written during the course of their study—students presented their community with a valid measure of their learning. Through the particular stories they chose, students informed their community about the range of the growing-up experiences of young people who live within it. They also invited their community to consider how those experiences influenced their lives—how they contributed to their development into adulthood.

To *The Bridge*, the collection of narrative essays that our students published, Gilbert contributed the following, an integrated statement about a number of the issues and concerns he investigated during the *Inquiry and Expression* course. He titled the statement "It's A Cold World," and claimed authorship of it in the table of contents by what I did not know until then was his given name, Gilberto Sanchez.

Parents are always telling you to do this and that and they say, "You better start thinking of your future." My mom would take me and my older brother to work in the fields, cutting weeds and separating cabbages, and we would earn our money there. Working there made me realize I needed to think of my future, to think of my goals in life. My mom was right. Working there made me realize I was becoming an adult even though I was still young. Maybe you could call it maturing.

It seems like problems started coming up the summer I was fourteen years old, when I started thinking of my future. When the season ended for working in the fields, I told my mom and dad I wasn't ever going back. That job wasn't for me. It was hard working there with the sun beating down upon your back and all those mosquitoes and bugs. I wasn't going back for sure. It was kind of traditional for our family to work there. My parents had to work there for a living for a while. When they were small, they would work in the fields to help my grandparent's finances. But now it was different, we would go so that our parents could teach us how to work hard for our money.

After a while my parents got on my case about my being lazy. They complained that I should be working, telling me I needed a job. I decided to go and fill out some applications. I applied at Little Caesar's Pizza. I knew a friend there, and he told me he could get me in. He was my girlfriend's brother and also my friend. We all grew up together, playing football in the neighborhood—me, my brother and all our friends. Within a week Little Caesar's called me and told me that I could start working the following

Wednesday. I was so excited and happy. My mom thought I'd never get out of the crib. Everything was going great, so I thought.

But it wasn't. My brother Robert had moved out of the house and gone into the army. He had been gone for just a week, and I already missed him. Ever since he left, the pressure has been on me. I have had to be the older brother. I have had to be a model for my little brother, Ruben. I have had to make sure I make all the right moves in front of my little brother. You know what I'm saying? Because I know that everything I do, Ruben will look at it is right. Because I never do anything wrong, is what he thinks. I have had to face up to the fact that I am the older brother and that I have to make my own decisions. All my life, I followed my older brother and did what he did and did what he told me to do. It's scary at times being the older brother.

Things get worse. My girlfriend moved out of town. My girlfriend Tina's pop got a better job offer. He's an electrician. His getting a better job offer was good. Nothing was wrong with that, but the job was out of town. Their family ended up moving to Holland, Michigan. I remember when Tina used to live down the street from me. I could just run down there and give her a little kiss. Now I have to save my hard-earned money and drive three hours to go to see her for the weekend. Her parents let me visit her, meaning they don't mind me visiting for the weekend and staying the night.

I think of Tina a lot. We can tell each other everything, solve each other's problems. We can talk to each other. She is the only one I can talk to about what I face everyday. She can make me feel so at ease, so secure. Life is much easier to handle with someone to share it with. You have that someone to rely on, you know what I mean?

Now that she moved, I think of how we will live our lives together. We are both changing into different people. She's making her plans, and I'm making mine. Each of us is trying to make our plans fit together. The change in ourselves—the way she's changing, and the way I'm changing—makes it hard to relate sometimes, and it worries me. We keep in touch. I call her, and she calls me, and we run up the phone bill. I'm in love.

When I started work, I did pretty good. Working there was all right. I didn't plan on saying there long. I find when I go to work, I'm not thinking of work, but of all the problems I face. Working can be a problem in itself. There are times we get so busy that everyone working is behind in their work, and everyone just has a mean look on their face. I sometimes have to work this huge oven cooking pizzas. The managers yell, people scream that they need help. No one can help because they need help themselves. It's hectic sometimes working there, especially when you are not thinking of work.

I started thinking about how work interfered with my friends because we would like to hang out sometimes. One of my friends, Pete, had asked me the first day of work if we were going out. I told him I had to work, but he understood. One Friday I asked for time off and the manager said, "Okay." So me and my boys went out to a football game. We were all walking like we were "bad," just chillin', and this guy came up to me and he started to front me. He had been wanting to fight me since the eighth grade and three years had passed since then. He started talking his shit. Now this guy thought he was bad. He thought he could kick my ass. I was a little scared, but then again who isn't when they are getting ready to fight.

While he was talking, I reached into my coat pocket and felt a lock so I grabbed it like a weapon. He had all his friends with him and I had all my boys with me and me and my boys are real close. It's like we are all brothers. We are blood, and blood's thicker then water, know what I'm saying? I told the guy, "Look, you want to fight, let's go then," and I cocked my fist back with the lock in my hand and hit him and the hood part of the lock, holding it like brass knuckles. Aiming for the face, I hit him. I'm pretty sure I busted his nose. He went down for the count, and this guy tried to hit me. I kinda moved out of the way and my boy, Ken, hit him with a right. Pete came in and hit him with a left hook, and Monty came through the crowd and blasted him in the face and that dude was through. This all happened in a split second. There was a big fight because we didn't stop. We kicked ass that night. We got a couple of blows from them, too. Well, at least I know I did, cause I remember going home in pain. My ribs were kinda bruised. That was a rough night that night.

The next week I went to see Tina, and I told her what happened. She was a little upset, not that I fought, well, that too, but mainly because I could have gotten hurt. She loves me, and I love her.

Life is hard when you're growing up, being a teenager. When I'm alone in my room, sometimes I stare at the wall and try to figure out my problems. Sometimes it seems there is no solution. Life is just beginning for me, but sometimes it seems to get harder and harder as I get older. The stress is always gonna be there, the problems, the trouble. I guess it's just something you have to live with. Growing up is hard to do; it's hectic sometimes. When it comes right down to it; you might want to say, "It's a Cold World."

Tawnya contributed a revised version of an essay she composed early in the school year, the narrative essay reproduced earlier in this chapter. In her revision of the essay, and perhaps of the events she recorded in it, Tawnya composes unfolding events with dramatic immediacy and omits the moral of the story that she chooses to entitle simply "Counting Money."

One day, my mother, my father, and I were getting ready to leave home. We were going to the children's zoo. We had our coats on. My mother had given me some change. When she gave it to me, she told me how much it was. I was so excited about going to the zoo, I ran to my father, showed him the change and I told him how much it was. He asked me to count if for him. I counted the number of coins. When I reached the last coin, I said the amount of money I had.

My father looked at me with an unhappy face and said, "No dear, try again." He took my hand and led me into the living room. He took a lamp off one of the end tables and spread the coins on the table. He looked at me and repeated, "Try it again."

He kept asking me to count the money. I would try to count the money once again. I would start crying. He would spank me for crying. Make me be quiet. But he kept making me count the money.

My father had everyone take their coats off. He said we were going to forget the zoo. he told me that unless I counted the money right, I would miss the elephants. I looked at him and said, "But why, Daddy."

He said, "Learning to count is more important than feeding the animals at the zoo." I began to try harder and harder, but the harder I tried, the more confusing the money became to me.

Once I counted the money correctly, he kept making me count it again and again. After he was sure I knew, he said, "Go lie down, and take a nap. It is too late to go to the zoo."

I went to my bedroom, put my head on my pillow, and cried silently because I knew I would be spanked again if he heard me crying. My two sisters were also upset because they didn't get a chance to go to the zoo. They said it was my fault.

My father left. Then my mother came into my bedroom, put her hand on my back, and said, "You can get up if you want to." I guess she felt sorry for me counting that money all day and missing the zoo.

Students in the *Inquiry and Expression* course represented their school learning in a form that might inspire learning in their home community. Their work was in keeping with the course of the study in which they engaged. As they prepared a collection of narrative essays for circulation, they used the competencies they had developed in the English language arts to present the understandings of the growing-up experience that they had developed. Students working in dialogically developed curricula in other disciplines, interdisciplines, and subjects appropriately publish their learnings about other topics in other forms. For example, in science classes in which teachers named the Saginaw River as a topic of inquiry, students not only learned to conduct tests to determine the quality of water up and down the river's watershed, but they also noted their findings; mapped, charted, and graphed their findings; and wrote reports about their findings for various audiences beyond their classmates and teachers—for readers of their city newspaper, for officials in the Department of Natural Resources (DNR) in Michigan, for officials in the Environmental Protection Agency (EPA) in Washington, and for students and teachers around the globe involved in the Global Rivers Environmental Education Network (the GREEN). As they learned to conduct scientific tests, keep science notebooks, and write scientific reports, students in these classes also learned science. They learned about the properties of river water and the organisms that live in that water under various conditions.

As in other dialogically constructed curricula, each science class' common study of the Saginaw River took particular shape in terms of particular students' particular concerns. Students in one class, for example, began to wonder what life forms lived in the mud under this river that had washed so much industrial waste into the nearby bay. They took mud samples, studied them under microscopes, and learned that in most of the river mud in the area of their city nothing lived. Students in another class decided that they would like to map the contours of the river floor. Standing side by side on a bridge that crosses the river in downtown Saginaw, they lowered weighted lines to the river bottom. Measuring the lines and graphing their measurements, they charted the river bottom. As it happens, they were the first scientists to do this.

Their inquiry produced original research that they published for interested agencies in the form of contoured maps of the river floor. Not surprisingly, students in science classes whose teachers invited them to identify and investigate their particular interests in the river most frequently chose to do so in teams and to publish their work collaboratively, just as their professional counterparts most frequently do. Although students in the *Inquiry and Expression* course followed the practice of most writers of imaginative literature when they published narrative essays they had composed individually, they also collaborated to select, organize, edit, and distribute *The Bridge.*

While the publication of students' work is not uncommon, particularly in composition courses, *The Bridge* and publications like the maps of the Saginaw River floor and water quality reports that emerge from dialogic curricula are less common because they are designed to do more than display students' learnings: They are designed to invite learning and action in the communities in which students live. Because the work that emerges from a dialogic curriculum is based on students' prior experiences, it seems particularly fitting to recirculate it in the communities in which the seeds of those understandings originated.

Like the reports. maps, and charts developed in science classes, *The Bridge* called for and inspired response in the world. Writings composed by young people born and reared in a city in the northeastern United States during the 1970s and 1980s, who had a vested interest in telling their stories, are writings that deal with both difficult and pleasurable themes. *The Bridge* is a book about the problems of persistent poverty and racial discrimination as surely as it is about childhood pranks and the precious role that grandparents play in children's upbringing. In a very real sense it was not an easy book to compose or to publish. It required courage. Students who treated some of the most difficult themes and problems that young people in Saginaw associate with their growing up discussed their writing with their families and friends, whose responses to them were noteworthy. Parents, family members, and friends were proud of their young people's courage and accomplishments in "telling it like it is." They supported the authors of *The Bridge* in ways we could not have anticipated. One grandmother, for example, came all the way from Louisiana to the Authors' Party in the Montague Inn to honor her grandchild.

As learners in the *Inquiry and Expression* course hoped it would, *The Bridge* has informed and inspired learning and action in and beyond the Saginaw community. Shortly after its publication, *The Bridge* inspired teachers to argue successfully for co-teaching, heterogeneous grouping, and the development of dialogic curricula in secondary school English courses in Saginaw's high schools. On an on-going basis, it informs students in schools, colleges, and universities across the country who read it to learn about the experiences of urban youngsters growing up in the postindustrial northeastern United States and the meanings those youngsters made of their experiences.

During the year after its publication, it inspired a class of students in the school district's Center for the Arts and Sciences to stage a production of *The*

Bridge. Working with their teacher's adaptation of the book, these theater arts students dramatized a musical version of the book that highlighted the racial tension and loneliness that many *Inquiry and Expression* students experienced as they were growing up.[12] Sitting in the auditorium in which the play was produced in October 1989, I watched many of the students who composed *The Bridge*, as they watched others' interpretation of their work.

Later as I listened to these students' after-the-performance conversations, I learned an important lesson: The products of their learning that students publish during or as end products of dialogically developed curricula not only inspire others to learn and act but also inspire the students who produced them to continue to learn and act. Pleased and displeased with others' interpretations of their work, students wanted to clarify, redo, affirm, disagree: "I want to see how the paper reviews this tomorrow." "We should write our own review." "We should have written the script." "I'm going to write more poetry, maybe a whole book of it."

Watching their literacy at work in the world, *Inquiry and Expression* students wanted to continue to practice it. They wanted to continue to learn and act, to continue to inspire learning and action.

Dialogues Between Self and Other

Although the dialogues between teachers and students documented in this chapter illustrate the distinguishing characteristics of a dialogic curriculum, they do not demonstrate the quality of students' learning in such a curriculum. Illustrative examples do not add up to authentic evidence of students' learning. Anyone can "get lucky" or perform below his or her level of ability on one or another of the tests of learning that are usually given in schools. Only examination of multiple examples of a student's work can demonstrate his or her understanding and competence, and only a careful study of a student's work over time can demonstrate the change in understanding and competence. For this reason, the next chapter presents a case study of the work produced during the *Inquiry and Expression* course by one student—a student who was neither the most nor the least accomplished of her classmates and whose progress during the year one might call typical. I also present the case study to dramatize the second kind of dialogue that shaped the *Inquiry and Expression* course: dialogue in which students composed and responded to their own curricular invitations.

Notes

1. Throughout his essay "Discourse in the Novel," published in *The Dialogic Curriculum* (Austin, TX: University of Texas Press, 1981), the well-known collection of four of his essays, Mikhail Bakhtin discusses his theoretical construct, heteroglossia, in terms like these:

The authentic environment of an utterance, the environment in which it lives and takes shape, is dialogized heteroglossia, anonymous and social as language, but simultaneously concrete, filled with specific content and accented as an individual utterance. (272)

2. Throughout this book, when I have reproduced students' texts, I have been faithful to the original forms in which students submitted them to their teachers. For ease of reference, when students did not entitle their compositions, I have. I have distinguished between students' titles and mine by enclosing mine in brackets.

3. In his important book the *Pedagogy of the Oppressed* (New York: Seabury Press, 1970), Paulo Freire insists that teaching and learning consist in learners' purposeful construction of meaning and understanding, not in teachers filling empty vessels with imperial gallons of facts (and now, of course, readers will be reminded of the argument of Charles Dickens' *Great Expectations*).

4. E. D. Hirsch, Jr. *Cultural Literacy: What Every American Needs to Know.* (New York: Vintage Books, 1988).

5. Maxine Greene, *Landscapes of Learning* (New York: Teachers College Press, 1978): 18–19.

6. Greene, 18.

7. Shirley Brice Heath and Charlene Thomas, "The Achievement of Preschool Literacy for Mother and Child." In *Awakening to Literacy,* edited by Hillel Goelman and Antoinette Oberg (London: Heinemann Educational Books, 1984): 51–72.

8. David Bartholomae and Anthony Petrosky, *Facts, Artifacts, and Counterfacts.* (Portsmouth, NH: Boynton Cook • Heinemann, 1987).

9. Parts of this discussion have appeared earlier in Patricia Lambert Stock, "The Function of Anecdote in Teacher Research," *English Education* 25:3 (Oct., 1993):173–187.

10. See Jay L. Robinson and Bernard Van't Hul. *Real World English: Words; Real World English: Sentences; Real World English: Language Variation* (New York: Scholastic Books, 1978).

11. To encourage students' work, the Vice President for Minority Affairs in the University of Michigan, Charles Moody, provided desktop publishing equipment and technical assistance to teachers and students in the *Inquiry and Expression* classrooms. Students learned word processing and software programs designed to produce camera-ready text that might be reproduced and bound in the form of a paperback book.

Because this work was time consuming, students—many of whom had full-time jobs and children of their own at home—came to school early in the morning and for most of the day on two spring Saturdays.

12. Steve Weaver, teacher of theatre arts in the Saginaw Public Schools' Center for the Arts and Sciences, adapted and directed the well-received and well-reviewed October 1989 stage production of *The Bridge*.

2

Wendy Gunlock's Intellectual Project

She must learn again to speak
starting with I
starting with We
starting as the infant does
with her own true hunger
and pleasure
and rage.
      Percy, 1994, "Unlearning Not to Speak," in *Circles of Water,* 97

No one ever told us we had to study our lives,
      make of our lives a study, as if learning natural
history or music, that we should begin
      with the simple exercises first
and slowly go on trying the hard ones . . .
      Rich, 1981, "Transcendental Etude," in *Lesbian Poetry,* 17

Wendy was seventeen the year she was a student in the section of *Inquiry and Expression* that Jane and I taught together. In those days, she donned her soft-ball jacket and letter with pride. In class, she sat front row center, not because she chose to, but because Jane's alphabetical seating arrangement placed her there. During the second week of school, on a day when I was leading a class discussion, Wendy glossed my comments with her own mumbled commentary. Whenever I asked her to share her comments with the entire class, she refused. Wishing to nip what I perceived to be a disruptive habit in the bud, I suggested that Wendy either share her comments with everyone during whole class discussions or keep them entirely to herself. She slumped far down in her seat. Before class ended, she had stretched forward in her seat as far away from her classmates as she could manage within the confines of her desk-chair. Pulling her facial muscles taut, she crossed her arms purposefully and grasped the front of her desk with outstretched fingers; then, lowering her head onto her arms, she closed her eyes, and bowed out of the class session. My pointed remarks had caused her to lose face.

As Wendy was leaving class, I stopped her to say that I was sorry I had embarrassed her and to ask her if she realized that she had embarrassed me. Never meeting my eyes, she mumbled her irritation with me and left the room. In one of the electronic messages she sent to me in Ann Arbor that week, Jane indicated that Wendy felt I was picking on her.[1] I wrote Wendy a note from Ann Arbor to apologize again for embarrassing her, suggesting that my own shy, uncertain feelings in the Saginaw classroom, my fear of falling on my face in my new teaching situation may have caused me to be insensitive and unfair. I was really sorry. Would Wendy please excuse me? Wendy responded with a letter: She understood why I had "picked on her"; she guessed she had been giving me a hard time. I shouldn't worry about it so much. It was nothing.

It wasn't "nothing." It was an opening for Wendy to claim space in the classroom that was different from her assigned one—front row center. In part because I complicated my place in that domain, confessed myself able, in the role of disciplinarian, to make mistakes, Wendy could change her stance as I had. This was not to be a domain in which interactions were governed by fixed rules. Rather, teacher and student could invest their interactions with meaning by talking about them, writing about them, and alluding to them. Our dialogue had begun. Our actions, undertaken in language for one another defined a starting place for teaching and learning. Thereafter, when Wendy said, "Don't pick on me" or "You're picking on me again," and when I said, "Wendy, I need to pick on you for a minute or two," ours was meaningful, communicative discourse, defining footing for a productive relationship. Yet it was more than that. In our exchanges, we were talking teaching and learning, and we both knew it. As with most teachers and students, such talk was important. In Wendy's case it was important because she is shy, as embarrassed by praise as by criticism. For at least the first semester of our year-long study together, Wendy pulled as far as she could toward the peripheries of the classroom community whenever she was attended to in it, whenever she was recognized as other than a uniformed figure, whenever she was heard as speaking in other than half-swallowed glosses or retorts. It was also important for Jane and me. As we leaned toward Wendy to observe her, bent toward her to hear her, studied her texts to read her, we watched her tell the truth about her life as she understood it. Based on our observations we were able to respond to the intellectual work she was defining for herself; we were able to plan for her development as a reader and a writer.

Wendy Responds to Her Teachers' Curricular Invitations

We began our work to encourage Wendy and her classmates to identify the materials of a project they cared enough about to invest themselves in studying by asking them to write and discuss several informal compositions about growing-up experiences. During the first weeks of *Inquiry and Expression*, as she and her classmates recorded stories about growing up in their families, Wendy moved from rehearsing one of her grandmother's growing up stories (W-1), to recalling times when she fought and played with her brother (W-2), to reviewing the good times she had during family car trips (W-3), to reconstructing narrative descriptions of her relationship to her parents and her peers (W-4).

W-1—[The Outhouse]

I remember, it was rainy real hard & I had to go to the bathroom and back in my days we had to use the outhouses. Anyway I went out to use the outhouse to go to the bathroom & I was really tired that day because we had nothing to do because it was rainy so hard so I ran out to the outhouse & while I was waiting to the bathroom dozed off for about a ½ hour so my father was just getting his shoes on & when I woke up I hurried up & went in the house & my father said to me where in the hek were you. I was just getting my shoes on to look for you. We were getting worried. So I had told him that I fell asleep in the outhouse & he just started to laugh. They never let me forgot what happen.

W-2—[My brother and I]

I remember when I was growing up, me and my brother would always get into fights. I remember one night my brother's friends, Scott & Jim was spending the night they snuk into my room & they had taped a tape of scary noises & when I fell asleep they snuk under my bed & pushed play & all I could her alnight was scarey noises so finally I got so scared I ran downstairs & into my mom & dads room & fell asleep in their bed I also remember we were getting our house rebuild & I was upstairs in my brother's room & I was jumping on his bed & a nail was sticking out & when I was jumping and the nail got stuck into my head & I went to bed not knowing about it & when I got up the next morning to comb my hair, the comb could not go all the way through my hair I went downstairs to ask my mom what was in my hair & she hurried up & got my dad up & took me to the hospital & they took the nail out & I don't remember if it even hurt.

W-3—[Family Traveling]

I remember when I was growing up, we did a lot of traveling. We had a lot of friends out of state (still do) and we would go & visit when we had a chance. We were in almost every state except for by up in Maine (them parts). It was really beautiful. We would drive through all the states & see all the sights. I remember driving through Kentucky, & the road we was on was out in the country, so all you could see was fields & some old houses with barns and horses. After we would drive through & get to our friends house, we would get settled and then go out driving around in their state that they lived in. It was a blast. Especially in West Virginia because my parents friend lives on a big hill & it is steep to. Anyway heir house was really hilly. It was great. I also liked driving through Florida because their friends would drive us along the beaches so we could see the oceans & condomens. I Think I like Florida the best because it is hot, beautiful, & a lot of beaches. I have been to Florida about 5 to 10 times.,The last 2 times I went to visit my brother & his wife to be, and we would also visit my parents frend Chris & Jewel who live in Pensecola. But every time I went I had a great time. So the point is. Try to get to see as much as the U. S. as possible, because there is so much to see.

W-4—[Unrest at Home]

I remember when I was growing up about 3 people moved into my house when I was about 9 or 10. There was [my mother's friend and her two] kids. Whenever something was missing, they would always ask us if we knew where it was. Of course, I did not know nothing about it, but [my mother's friend's kids] did, so they would say they didn't know even when they did. My mom & [her friend] would always say nobody is leaving till we know who took whatever was missing. [One of the kid's] would always take things all the time. But I would get really mad because I couldn't leave the table because [he] would take it & he would always so he knew nothing about it. My mom would believe me, but I guess it didn't matter to much because I got yelled at & grounded. I was reall ticked off. Another time was when me & [him] got into a fight. It started out with me and my friend was outside sitting on the picnic table & [he] came out & threw some food at her, so I threw food back at him because he had no right throwing anything at my friends. So after that we got into a big fight & my mom & [her friend] came home & broke it up. We had to go in the house & tell them what happen, so I told them & [he] told his side & [my mother's friend] believed him & my mom believed me so she started to yell and she called me a Bitch so I took off & went over to my Dads for a couple of days. then her & my mom got into a big fight too, so she left for a couple days & my mom was really up-set, but I didn't understand why she blamed me for starting it when he started it, plus he is always getting into trouble. Everything blew away though; I came back & so did [my mother's friend] & she said if we got into another fight she would ship me off to my dad's & [him] to his dad's. I was hoping she would because I wanted to live at my dads anyway.

Writing in response to assignments that asked her to collect and compose a growing-up story told her by an adult in her family and to recall and compose several of her own growing up stories, Wendy wrote one draft each of the first four pieces. Although liberally seasoned with mechanical and usage errors and expressed in language more characteristic of her speech than of our expectations for her writing, these compositions fullfilled the task we had assigned students: to record growing-up stories that could be shared in class discussions to help students identify events, issues, people, and themes that they wished to make subjects of their study in the *Inquiry and Expression* course.

In September, as we read the first writings Wendy submitted to us, we suspected that she composed them hastily and with minimal concern for their literary quality. Both the character of her written work and the frequent questions she asked us about these first writing assignments—"Now, just what do you want?" "How long should the story be?" "When is it due again?" "How do I write it?"—led us to believe that Wendy's primary concern was that her work fulfill the letter, if not the spirit, of her teachers' requirements for it. She wanted to "hand in" what we wanted, when we wanted it. Wendy, like others in our classes, wanted to graduate.

Although we think she composed these first four writings to satisfy her teachers' early assignments, not to explore her own intellectual project, we found in Wendy's willingness to "play school" indications both of her existing and potential capacities and of her sense of how to undertake writing tasks. The analyses Jane and I developed of Wendy's first four compositions indicate how we were looking at her writing in September and October of 1987, through lenses shaped by the local assessment of students' writing that we had worked together with other colleagues to develop the year before, through the lenses of teachers who did not yet know Wendy and were meeting her through writing she composed to fulfill their assignments. Developed as Wendy was shaping her intellectual project and we were learning to read her texts, the analyses that follow demonstrate teachers "keeping school." I include them here for three reasons: first, because I believe they represent one kind of early reading that teachers make of students' compositions; second, because with them I am able to illustrate features of students' writing that we noted and addressed routinely throughout the *Inquiry and Expression* course; and third, because they provide an illustrative contrast to the readings of Wendy's texts that shape the bulk of this essay. These readings took shape within a dialogic curriculum in which both the writing and reading of them functioned as "meaningful, communicative discourse."[2]

Her Teachers Develop Instructional Plans in Response to Wendy's Work

Although the signals of phatic communion, the *um*s and *ah*s of oral storytelling, are deleted from it, Wendy's first piece of writing (W-1), written in one six-sentence paragraph, reads like a transcription of a story her grandmother told her. Assuming her grandmother's persona, Wendy begins her narrative: "I remember, it was rainy real hard & I had to go to the bathroom and back in my days we had to use the outhouses." Then, as if to signal the beginning of the dramatic action of the story, she asks readers to attend carefully with, "Anyway. . . ." In so doing, Wendy seems to know that storytellers customarily provide their listeners/readers a context for the incident(s) that will shape the body of their stories, but she does not seem to know that a prefiguring reference in her first sentence (e.g., I remember a rainy day when I was young, back in the days when we had to use outhouses) or a backward glance from her second sentence to the first (e.g., One day I went out to use the outhouse. . .) would effect a more "literary" transition between these two parts of her story. Although the last sentence of her paragraph, her grandmother's closing comment: "They never let me forget what happen," together with the opening one of the piece suggest that Wendy knows that the dramatic action of stories customarily unfolds between an introduction (in this case contextual material) and a conclusion (in this case commentary), they are, at best, underdeveloped.

Further evidence that Wendy conceived her first piece of writing as a transcription of spoken language is found in the body of the narrative. First, she organizes the piece chronologically: "I went out. . ."; "While I was waiting. . ."; "when I woke up. . ." She tells the story, step by step, as it happened. Second, between the sentence-long introduction and the sentence-long conclusion that frame her piece, she marks typographically only four other sentences. Third, in one of these four, a ninety-word sentence, she writes more than half of her composition, using seven coordinating conjunctions (&, so, &, so, &, &, &) and four subordinating adverbs (because, because, while, when) to order and sequence the events of her narrative. In so doing, she captures the rhythms of informal, spoken language. Fourth, she makes extensive use of the ampersand (&) and the subordinating conjunction so, suggesting what might have been her effort in writing the narrative to keep up with the tempo of the story she was hearing. Finally, she fails to mark the direct speech she composes in her conclusion to the story: ". . .where in the hek were you. I was just getting my shoes on to look for you. We were getting worried." In response to this text, we did not specifically draw Wendy's attention to the "oral" quality of her writing, but we did engage her in the class discussions we were having about the differences between spoken and written texts in a way that we hoped would enable her to recognize herself that her first text read like a transcription of talk.

Although she begins her second composition (W-2) like her first, as if in response to her request to someone to recall a growing-up incident ("I remember when I was growing up, me and my brother would always get into fights."), this time Wendy is the person doing the recalling. She is not inscribing someone else's speech; she is composing her own. Written in two long typographical sentences, one of which is almost 400 words long, Wendy continues to make extensive use of the ampersand to relate events in her story to each other. (Her use of the conjunction so, which communicated the tempo of spoken language in her first piece, is almost absent here; the one time she does write the word, she uses it as a subordinating, not a coordinating conjunction: they played the "scary noises" so she "got scared" and "ran downstairs.") As we read, we noted that Wendy might easily have translated the long run-on constructions in this piece into a number of conventional sentences were she to delete the ampersands and replace them with more conventional punctuation. At the time she composed W-2, however, we questioned whether Wendy controlled the conventions for punctuation, usage, and the arrangement of written language that would allow her to coordinate, subordinate, or superordinate units of thought to one another as she might wish to do in her written compositions. Therefore, we planned to raise our question with her when her compositions provided us specific textual occasions.

When we first talked with Wendy about this second piece of writing, we drew her attention to the effectiveness of her overuse of detail to create apparent danger—"snuk in my room," "taped scary noises," "snuk under my bed," "all I could her alnight was scarey noises so finally I go so scared I ran downstairs & jumped into my mom and dads room . . ."—and her underuse of detail to express real danger—". . .I was jumping and the nail got stuck into my head & I went to bed not knowing about it. . . & they took the nail out & I don't remember if it even hurt." We also called her attention to the more effective way in which she related the body of her second piece of writing to its introduction than the way she had related the body of her first piece of writing to its introduction. For ourselves, we noted that the body of W-2 did not fulfill Wendy's introductory promise for it. The piece was not about fights with her brother, but rather about two frightening experiences in which she and her brother were involved: one in which her brother and his friends pulled a scary prank on her and another in which she and her brother were roughhousing together. Our notation led us to add another lesson to the instructional plan we were developing for Wendy. When appropriate, we planned to invite her, in class discussions or in writing conferences, to illustrate generalizations with examples and to compose generalizations about examples. In September we read students' writing and tailored our plans for writing instruction with specific students in mind.

By the time she submitted her third piece of writing to us, Wendy had not only heard several stories her classmates told about growing up, but also had read a number of handwritten versions of these stories distributed in xeroxed copies for discussion in small groups and with the entire class. She had also read and heard read aloud the growing-up stories of published authors. These spoken and written narratives perhaps influenced her written account of her family's car trips (W-3); certainly we hoped they would. Composed in two paragraphs and 18 sentences, this piece has both a one-sentence introduction that prepares the reader for what follows and three exemplified generalizations ("We would drive through all the states . . . with barns and horses"; "After we would drive through & get to our friends house . . . . It was great"; and "I also liked driving through Florida . . . But every time I went I had a great time.") Furthermore, Wendy marks a difference she wishes to communicate between the significance of her visits to Florida and those to Kentucky and West Virginia by discussing her visits to Florida in a separate paragraph. Although we believe that the paragraph's beginning might more appropriately start with the last sentence of her first paragraph, we were pleased to observe that Wendy recognized that a new paragraph would communicate her meaning more effectively. Adding to our sense that Wendy was working toward a more comprehensive grasp of how to make a written text in W-3, we noticed that for the first time, she used commas to signal relationships of word units to one another within sentences—twice appropriately (l. ?; l. ?) and twice inappropriately (l.?; l.?).

As her teacher-readers, we thought the weakest part of W-3 was its two-sentence conclusion: "So the point is. Try to get to see as much as the U. S. as possible, because there is so much to see." Wendy's use of *So the point is,* like her use of *Anyway* in W-1, provided us more evidence for our hypothesis that she was either not able or not working to effectively relate chunks of thought to one another with consistency. Her writing also led us to question whether Wendy was conceiving her writer's task as that of pleasing the teacher, that of meeting her assignments. We wondered if her use of the construction *So the point* is signaled nothing more meaningful than her uncertainty about whether or not her narrative fulfilled a school assignment. Did she sense that something general, something factual, should be offered to fulfill our assignments? Was hers a growing-up story? Should it have been something else? A travel log? An essay on the benefits of travel? On the greatness of America? After composing her own narrative, did Wendy wonder what uses it might have, what meanings it might communicate, in the school-world she occupied?

When Wendy composed the fourth and last piece of writing she submitted to us in September (W-4), we were concluding our inquiry into the similarities and differences between the modalities of speech and writing, the genres that contrast these two modalities of language use, and the values that attach themselves to such contrasts in literate societies. As we were doing so, we were encouraging students to allow their writing about the growing-up theme to enable them to write about topics in their own lives. Wendy responded with W-4, a narrative of personal experience; a narrative whose topics contrast sharply with those in W-1, W-2, and W-3; a narrative that seems located not in a fixed past but a changing present. As teacher-readers, we had something new to which to respond, a new world to interpret.

Wendy's new text, our new text, had some old things in it: It is composed in one paragraph, and although its sentences are more consistently marked as such, its units of meaning cry out for shaped elaboration. It is characterized by inconsistent punctuation and usage, a persistent problem in Wendy's writing. Still, it has shape: an introduction, a body, a conclusion. Wendy offers us some context for the incidents she narrates, though one that is underwritten if we are to judge their meaning within it, the familiar: "I remember when . . . " However, she helps us to understand their meaning by suggesting a mood that expresses her, not her teachers' presumed, reactions to the events she is telling: "I would get really made"; "I guess it didn't matter to much"; "I was reall ticked off." And she provides a necessary resolution to her proffered dramatic incident, "Everything blew away though; I cam back and so did [my mother's friend] . . . ."

Most noteworthy perhaps is the conclusion. It is strikingly different from those in W-1 and W-3. W-1, for example, closes the narration in the past: "They never let me for got what happen." W-3 closes even more surely with a piece of hortatory advice so general as to have no meaning in relation to personal experience: "So the point is. Try to get to see as much as the U.S. as possible, because there is so much to see." But in W-4, after giving postclosure to a narrated incident, "Everything blew away though; I came back and so did [my mother's friend]," Wendy opens the discourse again following another of her characteristic ampersands:

> & she said if we got into another fight she would ship me off to my dad's & [him] to his dad's. I was hoping she would because I wanted to live at my dads anyway.

We had to read Wendy's next text to fully realize how open this ending was and is, and to gain a sense of what kind of an opening it might prove to be. Textually, it does not work as well as some readers might want it to; intertextually, it led us to speculate about Wendy's potential as a developing writer.

At this point in October, we read W-4, in spite of its demonstration of persistent problems, as Wendy's best writing, perhaps because in it she introduces a problem that concerns her, one that she may wish to study. Still, we did not ignore the problems in this piece because we were as committed to Wendy's growth as a writer as we were to her growth as a researcher. In our developing instructional plan for Wendy, we decided to use appropriate occasions to explain to her the reasons a writer might choose one word over another, one sentence design over another, one paragraph placement over another. We decided not to recommend particular choices to Wendy because we wanted her to develop the practice of thinking about language choices. We did not want her to form the habit of writing into her compositions every suggestion we made to her. Furthermore, we did not want to constrain Wendy's use of writing to shape an intellectual project of importance to her by narrowing her attention to focus on features of texts that she might more readily produce later in the academic year.

Wendy Pursues Her Own Curricular Invitations

Having introduced several themes in her writing during the first month of the course—her relationships to her parents, her relationships to her peers, and her family traveling experiences—Wendy explored these interrelated themes during the next three months in a dialogue she established with the thoughts she was thinking, the things she was saying, and the texts she was writing. This dialogue between herself and the textual self she was composing began to take shape in three full-length essays, each of which she composed and revised over a month, and each of which she published for review within our classroom community. Having Wendy and her classmates to do three things: (1) to work independently and in small groups, using reading and writing to investigate the nature of particular growing-up experiences that concerned them and the stories individuals tell about those experiences; (2) to read three full-length works of published literature in which one or more of their particular concerns was a primary theme and to write critiques of these works; and (3) to compose three of their own growing-up experiences into literature that explored their particular concerns, we established a three-month workshop in our classes to provide students class time to do the work.[3]

Depending on their individual needs and interests, for two or three class hours each week, students engaged in sustained silent reading. For the remaining two or three class hours each week, they wrote about their own growing-up experiences and shared their writings and their reactions to their readings in pairs, in small peer-group meetings, and in whole-class discussions. The only assignments we imposed on students during these three months of reading-and-writing workshop study were a timetable of due dates for three book reviews and three carefully crafted growing-up stories. We teachers conceived our role in the classroom as advisors, consultants, counsellors, and most importantly as learners—students of our students' developing literacy and literature.

We enacted our role in the classroom dialogically. We talked with one student about a piece she was writing; with another about a book he was reading; with one small group about an issue they were addressing in common; with another small group about a growing-up story one of us had written; and so on. Each day in our classes, some students were reading or writing by themselves in chairs that faced the rear wall of the room; some, in small circles in front of the windows were reading drafts of their compositions and receiving responses to those drafts; some, in small circles in front of the book closets were discussing books they were reading. All were pausing from time to time to talk about their daily concerns, the latest news. Students and teachers were shaping language and referring to language they had already shaped to converse with one another, to reason with one another, to plan with one another, and to learn from one another.

During these months, students explored issues for study that concerned them. In the writing she composed during October (W-5), drafting and discussing her developing drafts with her peers—particularly with her friend Toni, Wendy followed her own curricular invitation to explore her relationship with her father, the one in her opening closure of W-4: "I was hoping she would because I wanted to live at my dads anyway."

At this time, instead of asking us "How long do you want this essay to be?" or "How many pages do I have to read today?" Wendy was developing and pursuing her own expectations for her work. As we watched her take charge, take responsibility for her own learning, we stepped back—out of her field of vision, out of her way—for a time.

W-5—My Father

Me and my father were never really close or nor was he close to my brother, Steve. We would never really talk or do anything when he was sober, but when he was drunk, it seemed like we were the perfect family.

My father was an alcoholic, a bad one too. He would drink until he woke up untile he had to go to work. He woke up at around ll:00 am and he would leave for work at 2:00 pm. Then he would drink after he got out of work. He did this 6 days a week, and on Sunday we would just drink all day.

My father was an alcoholic for about three years, then he quit for about five years, until his dad died on my brother's birthday. Then he started drinking again. His drinking had been getting worse. Finally, one day I was outside with my cousin Kris playing ball. My parents were in the house talking. My mother called me in the house and told Kris to go home. When I came into the house I say my dad getting ready for work, when he left, he didn't give my mom a kiss good-bye like he use to.

My mom told me to sit down because she had to talked to me. When I sat down I asked her what was wrong. She said how would you feel about me and your father getting a divorce. I told her that I would be mad and I didn't want my dad to leave. I guess she never took in what I felt about them getting a divorce. While they were still separated, my moms friend moved in with her 2 kids. A boy and a girl.

While they were separated my dad had moved in with his mother. The divorce finally came through. They had been divorced for 7 or 8 years. When my dad moved out his drinking had been getting worse.

When my mom's friend moved in, me and my older brother never knew why until a couple of months later. They had been living with us for about 10 years. When I was older, because of the situation at my house I wanted to go and live with my father, but I wasn't sure if I wanted to live with an alcoholic. I never moved in with him, but I was scared to. So I never did.

When my brother was old enough to move out he signed up for the Navy. When I think about him joining the Navy, "I say to myself" He was the smart one.

I would always go over to see my dad on the weekends. I only say him once a week. I wanted to see more of him, but I couldn't because I got out of school at 3:00 pm and he would leave for work at 2:00 pm.

When I did visit him, all he did was drink. All day, beer after beer.

I remember one weekend I spent the night. Of course, he was drinking. It got to be so bad, that he opened a beer, drank half and he struggled to go to the refridgerator to get another. So he had 2 beers. I got up poured both cans down the drain. I was so upset I left his house around 1:00 am and went back home. After that incident I went back over there the day after. When I arrived he was still sleeping. When he woke up, he never knew that I had left.

His drinking became so bad, my mom and her friend took my dad into the hospital because of his drinking and he had a bad back. When we took him in the hospital he was drunk. Ever time I went to the Hospital, he would be asleep. When he was better, we took him out of St. Lukes and transfered him to community Hospital, hoping that if he was in a alcoholism center he would stop drinking. he was in community for a month. I would go and visit him every day. He would show me around & we would just talked. That was the first we evr had a conversation. When he got to leave the hospital, I finally got up the nerve to tell him how proud I was for him to stop drinking. When I told him, he said that drinking is very dangerous. It can kill you & it almost killed me.

Ever since he got out of the Hospital, he hasn't touched a drop of alcohol. It has been about a year since he drank. Now all he drinks is pop & coffee. I am so happy that he quit. Now his life is back together & even though he doesn't have my mom, but he does have a son and daughter who loves him very much.

The product of between 8 and 12 hours of writing, discussion, and revision, this well-developed essay is a picture of the writing Wendy was composing by November. Its global organization is effective and serves Wendy's purpose: to describe her father from the perspective of her lived life as his daughter. In the first paragraph, she expresses straight forwardly,without self-pity, a sad reality of her life with her father: "Me and my father were never really close or nor was he close to my brother, Steve." In a second paragraph, she names why she was unable to be close to her father: he "was an alcoholic, a bad one," and she elaborates on her definition of a bad alcoholic. In a third paragraph, continuing with the elaboration she has begun, she gives a history of her father's alcoholism. Beginning with the fourth paragraph of the piece, she dramatizes the impact of her father's alcoholism on the life of her family, indicating her reaction when her mother asks her how she would feel about her parents' separation and divorce: "I told her that I would be mad and I didn't want my dad to leave." With the understatement we have seen before in her writing (W-2), Wendy reflects: "I guess she never took in what I felt about them getting a divorce."

In three more paragraph-length units, Wendy describes the implications of the divorce for her father, her mother, her brother, and for herself. In the eighth, ninth, and tenth paragraphs, she describes her weekend visits with her alcoholic father, and she dramatizes an especially painful one. In an eleventh paragraph, she accounts for the crisis that leads to her father's hospitalization for alcoholism, her daily visits to see him, and the first conversation they ever had. With poignant understatement, Wendy inscribes her effort to define her relationship with her father: "When he got to leave the hospital, I finally got up the nerve to tell him how proud I was for him to stop drinking." Similarly, she records her father's effort to build a relationship with her: "When I told him, he said that drinking is very dangerous. It can kill you & it almost killed me." As reflective readers we heard a generalization: "Try to get to see as much as the U.S. as possible, because there is so much to see." Yet how differently grounded these words are.

In a final paragraph, Wendy concludes her essay with a summary of her father's life since his hospitalization: "Now his life is back together. . . ." Caring about Wendy as a writer, and increasingly about Wendy herself, since she had begun to open her self to our view, we wondered about her ending to this narrative: What is its genre? Fairy tale? Realistic fiction? Is there a happily ever after like the ones Wendy is finding in the young adult novels she is reading during the time she is writing this essay?[4] What choices might Wendy have about the ways she might narrate her life? Our shaping questions began in turn to shape our instructional plans within the dialogic curriculum that Wendy now was developing with us.

Although the effectiveness of the global organization of her writing is not matched at the local level—an ability to control words, phrases, sentences, and groups of sentences—this piece of writing is a dramatic improvement over the four impromptu pieces she composed during September and October. Wendy is still composing occasional constructions like these: "Me and my father were never really close or nor was he close to my brother, Steve"; "I never moved in with him, but I was scared to"; "Now his life is back together & even though he doesn't have my mom, but he does have a son and daughter who loves him very much." More frequently, however, she is composing constructions like these: "When I was older, because of the situation at my house I wanted to go and live with my father, but I wasn't sure if I wanted to live with an alcoholic"; "When he was better, we took him out of St. Lukes' and transfered him to community Hospital, hoping that if he was in a alcoholism center he would stop drinking."

Until she undertook these assignments, which required revising, and until we were persuaded that she wished to communicate with her readers, we had not discussed with Wendy her errors in usage (e.g., her opening construction, "me and my brother") or mechanics (e.g., her use of quotation marks in W-5: . . . Navy, "I say to myself" He was the smart one). Now, when she seemed engaged and had ample opportunities to revise her work before submitting it to us, we included discussions of usage and mechanics in our writing conferences. But these discussions, not surprisingly, given the openings she had offered us, always followed discussions of the meaning she was making for herself and for us with her writing. They always followed discussions of the discoveries she was making in and with her texts and the ways she was finding and using language to achieve insight and balance to relate the facts of her life to one another and to the larger study in which we were engaged in the *Inquiry and Expression* course. Taking our lead from openings she provided us, at this time in the school year, our primary instructional goals for Wendy were to continue to help her explore the relationships between and among the ideas she was expressing in her writing and to focus her attention as she was reading young adult novels on how other authors gave literary shape to themes and events that concerned her.

As we studied the next piece of writing Wendy wrote, a growing-up story about the traumatic illness of her good friend, Tammie, we concluded that she was interpreting and exploring a curricular invitation that our plans for our course of study had provided her: an invitation to inquire into the forms and uses of language.

W-6—[Tammie]

I remember when I was downstairs watching television and all of a sudden the phone rang. It was my best friend's sister, Candy. She called to tell me that Tammie, my best friend was put in the hosptial about an hour ago.

I asked Candy why Tammie was admitted to the hospital and she told me that Tammie had a brain tumor. As soon as I hung up the phone and ran upstairs and started to cry, I had never been so upset before.

I finally calmed down and and came down and told my mom and her friend Sandi, we were all shocked about the horrible news.

I mean who ever thought that a close friend that I grew up with and who is like a sister could have a brain tumor. The doctor had said that she could of been borning with it.

I never knew how to deal with a friend having a tumor. All the time she was in the hospital, I would try to go up and see her as much as possible, unless I had to go to work. When I was at work, I would call and ask her how she was feeling.

Every time I called her and ask how she was, and she always said she was fine, but I really thought something was wrong.

I always thought of her as my best friend. Sure we had plenty of fights, we once even had a fist fight, but we would always work it out.

I always wanted to tell her that I cared for her and thought of her as a sister I never had. When I first found out about the tumor, I wanted to tell her even more, but I never could spit out the words.

One day I asked her how she was handeling having a tumor and she said that it really didn't matter and that she didn't care, but I think deep down inside she does care. I also had asked her if she is going to live through it. I asked her if she was scared and she said no, but I know for a fact she is was. Now she is having fun, going out to parties, and everything.

One rainy day in March, she collapsed on the dining room floor while I was spending the night. Her mother hurried up and called an abulance, they came to her house and took her to St. Lukes hospital. She was in coma for about 2 weeks. I was up to see her every day of the week, unless I had to work, and when I was working I would call. Every day I was up there hoping that she would come out of coma, but she never did. We were up to the hospital every day until visiting hours was over with.

One day I was there all by myself and I was just sitting their watching my best friend almost near death. All of a sudden I started talking to her, and I found myself telling her how much I loved her as a friend, and that I cared for her. I started to say that she was going to pull through this crisis because she has plenty of friends to help her pull through it. Then I started to say something about softball because we both live it, and I was holding her hand because I was so scared, and all of a sudden she started to move her fingers and I felt them moving. I looked up at her brown eyes and there she was just starring at me. I was so happy, I ran and told a doctor. he came in and examined her. He told me to call Tammie's parents, so I did. he told me to tell her parents to meet them in his office.

When the doctor left, I went back into her room. She was telling me about a dream she had. She said I was holding her hand and telling her that I loved and cared for her. "I said" it wsn't a dream, I said and meant evry word. She looked at me and she sat up and we just hugged each other. Now she's living a perfectly normal life.

Certain themes developing in Wendy's writing are immediately apparent to her responsive readers: her relationships to those she should and must care about—her family and her friends—and her fear of disability and death. As we read and talked about this and her earlier essays, another theme emerged: the role language plays in Wendy's relationships with those near and dear to her. In her writings, Wendy records talk only when she and her family or her friends have something difficult to report or explain. For example, in her essay, "My Father," when Wendy's mother tells her "to sit down because she had to talked to me," the talk is disturbing. The talk reports a divorce that Wendy does not want. Later when Wendy musters the courage to tell her father she is proud of him because he has stopped drinking, her father who "would never really talk or do anything when he was sober," speaks about drinking to her: "It can kill you & it almost killed me." In the essay about Tammie, the theme is even more dramatically treated and more integrally related to the topical subject of the piece—Tammie's unthinkable illness. When Wendy learns from a telephone call that her best friend is in the hospital, she asks "why Tammie was admitted to the hospital," and is "told . . . that Tammie had a brain tumor." This news is so up-setting to Wendy that she runs upstairs to cry. Finally, she comes downstairs to tell the news to her mother and her friend. "I mean who ever thought that a close friend that I grew up with and who is like a sister could have a brain tumor. The doctor said that she could been borning with it." The news she receives is news "who ever thought," news who would ever want to think in words; but Wendy communicates it in words and reports that it was explained in words.

Later in the essay, Wendy indicates that just as her father spoke neither with her brother Steve nor her when he was sober, she has never spoken to Tammie about important matters, such as the importance to Wendy of their friendship: "I always wanted to tell her that I cared for her and thought of her as a sister I never had. When I first found out about the tumor, I wanted to tell her even more, but I never could spit out the words." Instead, at this stage of her development, Wendy uses words most readily to report what is painful, upsetting: "One day I asked her how she was handeling having a tumor. . . . I also had asked her if she is going to live through it. I asked her if she was scared and she said no, but I know for a fact she is was." While Wendy's father's alcoholism may have made her "so upset that [she] left his house," her best friend's life-threatening illness is an event that must be confronted, understood, put some-how into a pattern of present living: Something not to be thought about because of the fears it evokes, it must yet be stated and its implications put into language for reflection. Wendy's father's alcoholism had been a similar problem for her to face; but it is his problem, one in part of his own making, the problem of a member of another, older, more distant generation, in psychological if not filial distance. And he did not live with her. Tammie's illness is closer to home, closer to heart, for Wendy: Tammie is her age, her best friend, close like a sister. If Tammie can have (can perhaps have been born with) a life-threatening illness, might not Wendy also become ill? Might not she also be vulnerable? Might not she also be mortal? These fears move Wendy to shape words, to ask painful questions of her friend, questions her friend averts, but questions Wendy knows her friend must contemplate because she must, too: ". . . she said it really didn't matter and that she didn't care, but I think deep down inside she does care. . . . I asked her if she was scared and she said no, but I know for a fact she is was."

Wendy's use of two verbs in this construction may well be precipitated by the fact that the reality she is writing about is so painful to her that she must get ahead of herself for just a moment as she composes this growing-up story; she must assure her readers, and herself, that Tammie's ordeal is a *was* not an *is*; it is over. The unthinkable may not have to be thought after all.

But before she puts the unthinkable to rest with the conclusion to her essay, before she gives it the fairy tale ending that she composes to the threatening story about one so close to her ("Now she's living a perfectly normal life."), Wendy finds another use for shaped language, one we did not read in her earlier writings. Exploring her relationship with Tammie, trying to give it shape and meaning, she composes it into a dramatic scene in which the actors have words to say to one another, even if those words can be reported only in indirect speech. In the scene she composes, Wendy sits with her friend Tammie, in the hospital, watching Tammie lying in a coma:

> watching my best friend almost near death. All of a sudden I started talking to her, and I found myself telling her how much I loved her as a friend, and that I cared for her. I started telling her that she was going to pull through this crisis because she has plenty of friends to help her pull through it. Then I started to say something about softball because we both live it, and I was holding her hand because I was so scared, and all of a sudden she started to move her fingers and I felt them moving. I looked up at her brown eyes and there she was just starring at me. . . .
>
> [Later,] she was telling me about a dream she had. She said I was holding her hand and telling her that I loved and cared for her. "I said" it wsn't a dream, I said and meant evry word. She looked at me and she sat up and we hugged each other. Now she's living a perfectly normal life.

At this point in her essay about Tammie, Wendy chooses to imbue language with restorative powers. She makes it the vehicle for communicating loving thoughts, no matter how complicated by their echoes of painful ones. Her words, in her remembering of them, in her capturing of them, bring about a miracle that is possible in the genre of fairy tale she is using to shape her narrative, fully consistent with a happy-ever-after that she expresses this way: "Now she's living a perfectly normal life," as if such a thing could be lived. But Wendy's magical words are rooted in a real world of remembered talk with Tammie: They come from and are evocative of shared space in the world, of things they value in common: "Then I started to say something about softball because we both live it"; and it evokes fears, and losses, presumed to be shared: "and I was holding her hand because I was so scared. . . ."

In thirteen paragraphs, nine of which are three or fewer sentences in length, Wendy juxtaposes bits of realized action with bits of felt reflection as if these bits were in dialogue with one another:

> I remember when I was downstairs watching television and all of a sudden the phone rang. It was my best friend's sister, Candy. She called to tell me that Tammie, my best friend was put in the hosptial about an hour ago.

I asked Candy why Tammie was admitted to the hospital and she told me that Tammie had a brain tumor. As soon as I hung up the phone and ran upstairs and started to cry, I had never been so upset before.

I finally calmed down and came down and told my mom and her friend Sandi, we were all shocked about the horrible news.

I mean who ever thought that a close friend that I grew up with and who is like a sister could have a brain tumor. . . .

At the same time that she creates a dialogue between action and reflection in this piece, Wendy sustains both, integrating them more effectively than she has in previous compositions, yet inevitably, leaving loose ends or strands that open toward new patterns. Wendy begins this essay, as she has not before, with action rather than preparation for action: "I remember when I was downstairs watching television and all of a sudden the phone rang." And she enriches her handling of the actions she presents with active predications and illustrative descriptions: "One rainy day in March she collapsed on the dining room floor while I was spending the night. Her mother hurried and called an abulance, they came to her house and took her to St. Lukes hospital."

During one of the writing conferences that Wendy and I had when she was composing "Tammie," I asked her if she watched afternoon television when she got home from school. She answered that she did not; she didn't like it, and anyway she had other things to do after school like practicing for the sports in which she participated. Explaining why I asked the question, I told Wendy that I thought I recognized the influence of "General Hospital" on her composition of the bedside hospital scene in "Tammie." After considering my statement, Wendy explained that although she was not a regular viewer she was familiar with "soap operas" and had seen enough of them to have images of them in her mind. She thought the genre had probably influenced her shaping of the hospital scene she composed because the scene was the product of her imagination, her friend Tammie did not have a brain tumor. "Tammie" was a fiction of Wendy's composition.

Influenced by both the young adult novels she was reading and the television programs we assumed she was watching, in W-6, Wendy is composing vividly imagined sequences of events. Among them, language itself figures as an event that can have consequences, consequences that make for openings, not closings, for coming together, not separation:

Then I started to say something about softball because we both live it, and I was holding her hand because I was so scared, and all of a sudden she started to move her fingers and I felt them moving. I looked up at her brown eyes and there she was just starring at me.

As we read and reread, we thought Wendy had found other reasons to use language as a way to shape both a world and a place in it. And, of course, we still read as her teachers. In her composition, Wendy incorporates strategies at the local level to enable herself to move between dramatic action and explanations and reflections: She replaces her too-easy use of transitions like *anyway* with more effective ones like *all of a sudden*. But while her movement back and forth at the local level between action and reflection are improved in this piece, her movement between the time in which she sets her text and the time at which she writes it is less effective. Like many developing writers, Wendy has difficulty communicating the differences between actions that precede the time defined by her textual time and the time in which she is writing her text. For example, in the first paragraph, she writes: "She called to tell me that Tammie, my best friend was put in the hospital about *an hour ago* (emphasis mine)" rather than *an hour before*; in the sixth paragraph, she writes: "Every time I called her and *ask* how she was. . .," rather than: "Every time I called her and *asked* how she was. . .," In the ninth paragraph, she writes: "I asked her if she was scared and she said no, but I know for a fact she is was," leaving two verb forms in her sentences as if she were unable to determine whether she herself were operating in the time of the text or the time in which she was composing it. In her confusion of tenses—of times—we read, a crucial moment in Wendy's development as a researcher and a writer. We construed the problems Wendy was having marking time in her writing as important problems that were integrally related to the research she was doing. We wanted to continue to explore the dimensions of the research project she was conceiving and to support her developing inquiry of the past in the present. We wanted to encourage her as she invested past experiences with present meanings with potential future uses. For these reasons, we did not call her attention to features of her writing that might have been construed as "errors," features such as her misuse of tenses in W-6.

During December and January, when she turned to write again about a subject and theme that she had written about earlier, family traveling (W-4), Wendy does not compose a travel log, naming places where she has traveled, but actually composes a story that focuses on what she and her companions did during a family camping trip. The complexities and implications of relationships preoccupy her at this stage in her development:

W-7—Going Up North

When I was little, about 4 or 5. My family and I went up North a lot. We belonged to a camping club called Timbertowns Travelers. (Thats what they called Saginaw back then.) We would go camping almost every weekend during the summer time. Their were about 10 families in the group all together. We had a great time when we went up North. we would have potluck dinners & go trick or treating to all the trailers on Halloween.

I rember one cold day in August, we had gone to Tawas City to go camping with our club. We had past a lot of frozen ponds on the way up there. Their was our family and the Martin's who would kind of like hang with each other.

The Martin's had 1 boy Mike and 2 girls, Rhonda and Kim. After we got settled down, me and my brother Steve went over to get Mike, Rhond, and Kim so we could go and get some thing to eat. We had left their trailer and didn't want to walk to get to the gate, so we decided to jump the fence to go to the A & W resternaut.

When we walked in, everybody just started to stare at us. we couldn't figure out why, so we kept on walking until we found an empty booth. After the waitress had taken our ordered, it was just 10 minutes before our food had arrived. After we got finished eating, Rhonda told me to put an A & W rootbeer mug under my hat. When I asked her why, "she said, She wanted to take home." I told her that I wasn't gonna do it, because I didn't want to get busted. She said that I wouldn't. I told her that something was wrong with her brain. I thought that the cold had something to do with it, but I finally gave in. I thought maybe something was wrong with my brain for stealing a mug. I qucikly put it under my hat & we left very swiftly & quickly. Then, as soon as we were out the door, I found myself running with a mug in my hand.

As soon as we got to the fence, we had to jump it to get back to the trailer park.

We went into our trailer and quickly shut the door. We all sat down and started to laugh, because we didn't get caught. After we had stopped laughing, we decided to play a fast game called Spoons. After we had played for a while, Mike was getting bored and decided to go ice fishing over to the pond.

When he was walking out the door, my brother Steve decided to go with him. So the both of left and Kim, Rhonda, and I decided to go sneak up of on them. We hurried & started following them. When Mike & Steve got to the pond, Mike was the 1st one on the ice. We were hidding by the bushes when we knew Mike had fallen into the water. We ran from the bushes where Steve was and him and Kim went to go get him but half way out there, Mike was standing in the middle of the pond drenched. He said the water only came up to his knees. We just suddenly bursted out laughing. They helped him out of the water and we hurried up to get back to the trailer so Mike could change.

We all took an oath saying we would never tell our parents, because they would kill us. Till this day, the still have no idea what all had happen that weekend, and probaby never will. When we look back, we will remember the great times we had with the Timbertown Camping Club.

In this piece, for the first time, Wendy is attempting to compose sustained dramatic action. In paragraphs four and seven of this eight-paragraph composition, she writes longer chunks of discourse than she has tried before. Within each, she describes the scene and actions of an adventure she, her brother, and their friends create when they are camping with their parents one cold day in Tawas City. As she experiments with new possibilities in her prose, Wendy writes energetically: "I quickly put it under my hat & left very swiftly & quickly"; "Mike was standing in the middle of the pond drenched." Rather than reporting talk indirectly as she did in "Tammie" (W-6), in this essay, Wendy uses talk both to provide her readers images of speaking persons and to lend her story the vitality of a drama. Furthermore, she creates her drama novelistically, coloring the events as Jerome Bruner tells us mature narrators do—by "subjectivizing" them, by depicting them "not through an omniscient eye that views a timeless reality, but through the filter of the consciousness of the protagonists in the story."[5]

> I told her that something was wrong with her brain. I thought that the cold had something to do with it, but I finally gave in. I thought maybe something was wrong with my brain for stealing a mug.

As in mature narratives, subjectivity (ways of looking toward a reality that must be constituted) constitutes multiple perspectives: Rhonda's view; Wendy's view; those of parents, of local residents, of police—all of whom would see the theft differently. Wendy's understated opening, used to set a context for the event she will narrate, invites model readers to think their own thoughts about perspectives, to imagine themselves in similar situations: "When we walked in, everybody just started to stare at us. We couldn't figure out why, so we kept on walking until we found an empty booth."

Reading these words in retrospect, thinking about perspectives, Wendy's narrative about theft becomes another kind of event: Did Wendy see that? We thought so, in our reading of the moves she makes in the composition. In an early move, Wendy reaches out to an audience imagined as distant from her, to readers who will need guidance to enter a personal world and its immediate constitutients: "We belonged to a camping club called Timbertown Travelers. ("That's what they called Saginaw back then."). She prefigures a central event in her narrative in offering early a temporal reference and a detail about the landscape: "I remember one cold day in August, we had gone to Tawas City to go camping with our club. We had past a lot of frozen ponds on the way up there." Her more vivid depiction of action, her use of words to represent speaking persons, fits into this landscape. Wendy is more vividly remembering and imagining her world; furthermore, she is giving it texture in a way that will help her readers imagine it and remember events of their own making in similar worlds.

Intertextuality: Wendy Works
with Others to Co-compose a Curriculum

At the same time that she was working to write and revise the essays "My Father" (W-5), "Tammie" (W-6), and "Going Up North" (W-7), Wendy and her classmates were discussing the growing-up stories they were composing and reading. She also was conferring several times a week with us about her reading and her writing. While it is not possible for us to know the extent to which class discussions, conferences with us, and her reading and writing were influencing one another, we are able to demonstrate that these activities were informing one another, even as they were informing Wendy's research.

A letter Wendy wrote to me early in the second semester of the course suggests the dialogue in which we were engaged at the time, one in which Wendy not only has a great deal to tell us about the things she does and thinks, but one in which she is confident that I am genuinely interested in what she does and thinks. Wendy describes a day-long field trip that *Inquiry and Expression* students took to Delta Community College (University Center, Michigan). During the day designed for visiting high school students, Wendy and her classmates attended three workshop/classes for which they had registered previously. In this section of the letter, Wendy describes the computer-skills workshop she attended:

> In the beginning of the class we booted up our computer with a disk & then we played a game so the teacher could see if she could remember all of the names in the class. You had to say "my Grandmother went on a trip and in that trip she packed in the trunk" & then we had to say our name then say a word that started with the same as your first name. I still remember all the names Craig-cabbage, Merisia & mayononaise, Heather Hotdogs, Pam-Pickles, Wendy Water, Ann & achovies, Mellissa & meat, Toni-tomatoes, Vincent Volume, Brenda-Beer- Angie Avocolos, Gavin goobers. Paulette Pancakes, Anita-apples Mike U Mustard. Plus there were Martha, Dexter & Kevin. But we didn't have enough time for them to say the phrase. then we made up a poem & then some people read it out loud & then we finished typing in a paragraph in the computer. Then she showed us how to delete words. & moving paragraphs. It was an easy class because I already knew how to do it. I really liked that class we had a Great Time.

Another letter Wendy wrote to me at this time demonstrates how she was relating the many dialogues in which she was engaged—class discussions, conferences with her teachers, her reading, and her writing—to each other. This section is a response Wendy wrote to a passage from Stephen King's quasi-autobiographical novella *The Body,* in which King's protagonist, Gordon LeChance is reflecting on "Stud City," the first story he wrote:

> No, it's not a very good story—its author was too busy listening to other voices to listen as closely as he should have to the one coming from inside. But it was the first time I had every really used the place I knew and the things I felt in a piece of fiction, and there was a kind of dreadful exhileration in seeing things that had troubled me for years come out in a new form, a form over which I had imposed control. It had been years since that childhood idea of Denny being in the closet of his spookily preserved room had occurred to me; I would have honestly believed I had forgotten it. Yet there it is in "Stud City," only slightly changed . . . but controlled. (King, *The Body,* 323)

When I invited Wendy to reflect on this passage in a letter to me, I expected she would comment on the control over events in their lives that authors can take by writing about them because we had been discussing that issue in class. I had not expected Wendy to identify herself as a creative writer, as a writer of dramatic stories even though she had composed a fictional piece in "Tammie" and crafted "Going Up North," as dramatic action.

In her letter to me, Wendy writes:

Well, I really think the story that Gordon wrote & the stories that I have wrote are quite the same as in to be similar in the creative writing. I think that they are the same as in writing because his story is dramatic.

His story is a story about what maybe he had experienced or someone he knew has experienced.

It's similar to mine because he had used his own words & his own thoughts. It is how he had experienced in his life & how he tells about it. I think he had control of his story because he could change things & rewrite them.

When Wendy claims that her writing is like LeChance's writing because it is creative writing, because it is dramatic writing, she indicates that she is attending not only to the content of the published literature she is reading but also to its shape.

In a letter she wrote to Zibby O'Neal, author of the young adult novel *In Summer Light*, Wendy gives us further evidence that she is reading, at this time, not just to inform her understanding of the themes that define her intellectual project, but also to inform her understanding of how to write about those themes. She also gives us evidence of the ease with which she is able to engage in dialogue about her intellectual project with adults who are not her teachers.

My name is Wendy Gunlock and I'm a Senior at Arthur Hill High School in Saginaw, Mich. Our 5th class . . . with our teacher Mrs. Denton were at the Delta College Writing Festival and our class heard you speak. I thought "In Summer Light" was boring in the beginning of the book, but towards the middle it became interesting.

I would like to ask some questions about how you ever got started to become a professional writer. How could you just sit down & write a whole book. Did you ever live or grow up in Massachusetts, is that why you had used this particular state. I just have 1 last question, "Do you really enjoy writing."

. . .

How can you make a story more interesting. My story is about my family and another who goes up north & has some kind of strange incidents. How can I make this story seem interesting for other students as well as adults to read and enjoy it like if they were there, going through what we all went through.

After introducing herself ("My name is Wendy Gunlock and I'm a Senior at Arthur Hill High School in Saginaw, Mich."), indicating her familiarity with O'Neal's work ("Our 5th class . . . with our teacher Mrs. Denton were at the Delta College Writing Festival and our class heard you speak."), and establishing herself as a critical reader of O'Neal's writing (" I thought "In Summer Light" was boring in the beginning of the book, but towards the middle it became interesting."), Wendy speaks to O'Neal, the experienced researcher/writer, from the perspective of a novice researcher/writer: "Did you ever live or grow up in Massachusetts, is that why you had used this particular state."

In a move that made us smile, we thought we also saw Wendy take on the serious task of speaking to O'Neal, researcher to researcher: "My story is about my family and another who goes up north & has some kind of strange incidents. How can I make this story seem interesting for other students as well as adults to read and enjoy it like if they were there, going through what we all went through."). In this paragraph of her letter, we read Wendy's saying: "Just as I need to learn about how to make my work interesting to adults like you, I think you need to learn how to make your work interesting to young people like me."

In addition to the evidence we found in her letters, we found still other indications of how Wendy's reading and writing were influencing one another in the book reviews she composed for us between October and February.[6] Although at first we read her book reviews as plot summaries, when we studied them within the intellectual project Wendy was pursuing in *Inquiry and Expression*, when we read and discussed the book reviews she wrote, in the light of the literature she was composing, we realized that in taking seriously the guidelines we offered her for writing her book reviews, she had chosen to "be informal," to "be chatty," to tell us how the books she was reading "spoke or did not speak to [her] about growing up." In her book reviews, Wendy provides us glimpses of the intertextuality of her reading and writing, glimpses of the "web of meaning" she was spinning with her reading and writing. They provide a window through which we might see how the young adult literature she was reading was informing Wendy's understanding of the themes she was studying and the genres in which research into those themes might be expressed.

Her review of Tommy Hallowell's *Varsity Coach* illustrates why we first read Wendy's book reviews as plot summaries:

W-8—Varsity Coach

The title of this book is Varsity Coach. The author is Tommy Hallowell. The book is about a young named Craig Brower, who is a junior at Kenmore Heights High School. Craig is a member of the Varsity football team, who is always the star halfback of his losing team under their coach. in Craig's sophomore year.

During the end of summer their is a ad in the newspaper about having football tryouts for the Varsity Squad under a new coach.

The new coaches name is Coach Cronin. He never played the sport of football, but knows everything to know about the game itself.

Craig Brower and his best friends all went to tryouts & all had made the team as expected. Craig was the man of team. He brought everyone up with his excitement & energy. Between both Craig & Coach Cronin they could turn Kenmore Heights into a winning team. But something happened to Craig. He noticed that his parents had been fighting alot, & it brang Craig down. Well Craig was getting ready for the first game of the season, when his parents started to fight. He tried to ignore it & get ready for the game, but somehow he couldn't doing. He was finally ready & left for the game. he was getting down about his parents fighting, but he was also excited about playing. He decided to get his parents out of his mind & get it on the game. and that he did. Even though Craig played his best effort, they still lost by a touchdown. After the game he went home & his parents had been fighting again. After listening to them, he ran upstairs & tried to get some homework done. He couldn't concentrate so he pulled out some Vince Labarda Football Volumes and started to read.

After the practice got over with he came home & his mom had told him to sit down, because she wanted to talk to him. She told Craig, that they were getting a divorce. Craig was so upset, he ran upstairs & slammed the door, trying to think about the next game. That he did. He went over all the plays "everything." He fell asleep & when he woke up his father was packing, told Craig that he would call later. And then he left, & Craig went upstairs to get ready for the game. The game was really & even though they won Craig was so upset he let it out the team for playing lousy.

After screaming at the team he went home and ate dinner after dinner he went out to shoot some baskets. His best friends came over Jim & Dave. They shoot baskets & talked about Craigs parents getting a divorce. Then they left & Craig went upstairs to go to bed. They won the rest of the season games. The had made it to the play-offs for the 1st time in 20 years. During the 1st play off game all the pressure was building up on Craig. Although he had a 120 yeard rushing & 2 touchdowns & they were still down by a touch-down Craig thought he hasn't played well enough. But with the ball on the 20 yeard line and 1.00 minute left it was 4 & 1. They couldn't get a field goal, because they still would be behind. So they gave the ball to Craig. His pressure had build up so bad that when he got the ball he broke through at least 5 tackles to get a 1st down, but he was still going on his feet & made a touchdown. The score was 14 to 13. Coach Cronin decided to go for it all & go for the 2 point conversion.

He knew that if the extra point was good it would be tied 14 to 14. but Craig told the coach he could get it, so the coach called the play & the quar-terback handed the ball to Craig once again like before, and the next thing Craig knew, he was in the end zone. He did. He made it & they won the game 15 to 14. After the celebration he talked to the coach about his parents After talking, the coach had straigten Craig out. He know understood everything. And know he is the team leader & they were off to the Championship game.

Closer readings of this and her other book reviews revealed the similarities between and among the texts Wendy was reading and the compositions she was writing between October and January. For example, her review of *Varsity Coach*, the story of a high school athlete whose parents' marriage is breaking up, ech-oes the essay she wrote earlier about her relationship to her father (W-5) and pre-figures one she will write later about her relationship to her mother (W-9).

In her composition "My Father" (W-5), Wendy positions herself as a ball-playing child who recognizes her parents' marriage is in trouble and is told that they plan to divorce:

My father was an alcoholic for about three years, then he quit for about 5 years, until his dad died on my brothers birthday. Then he started drinking again. His drinking had been getting worse. Finally, one day I was outside with my cousin Kris playing ball. My parents were in the house talking. My mother called me in the house and told Kris to go home. When I came into the house I saw my dad getting ready for work, when he left he didn't give my mom a kiss good-bye like he use to.

> My mom told me to sit down because she had to talked to me. When I
> sat down I asked her what was wrong. She said how would you feel about
> me and your father getting a divorce. I told her that I would be mad and I
> didn't want my dad to leave. I guess she never took in what I felt about them
> getting a divorce.

In her book review of *Varsity Coach* (W-8), Wendy's description of the
scene in which Craig Brower, the high school, ball-playing protagonist of the
young adult novel hears his parents fighting indicates that she read his experience in terms of her own. She empathizes with the protagonist of the novel;
she knows what and how he feels.

> After the game he went home & his parents had been fighting again. After
> listening to them, he ran upstairs & tried to get some homework done. He
> couldn't concentrate so he pulled out some Vince Labarda Football volumes
> and started to read.
>   After the practice got over with he came home & his mom had told him
> to sit down because she wanted to talk to him. She told Craig that they were
> getting a divorce. Craig was so upset, he ran upstairs & slammed the door,
> trying to think about the next game. That he did. He went over all the plays
> "everything." He fell asleep & when he woke up his father was packing, told
> Craig that he would call later, and then he left, & Craig went upstairs to get
> ready for the game. The game was really close & even though they won
> Craig was so upset he let it out the team for playing lousy.
>   After screaming at the team, he went home and ate dinner. After dinner
> he went out to shoot some baskets. His best friends came over Jim & Dave.
> They shoot baskets & talked about Craigs parents getting a divorce. Then
> they left & Craig went upstairs to go to bed.

In an impromptu essay she writes about her mother in January, Wendy retreats to the privacy of her bedroom to "think about what it would be like if. . . ."
just as Craig retreats to his bedroom to try "to think about the next game."

From W-9—[What Has Happened in My Life]:

> When my brother was old enough he joined the Navy. Know he is living
> with his bride to be. Sometimes when I am upstairs in my bedroom lying
> down on my waterbed, I just start to think about what has happened with my
> life. And what it would be like if my parents never got a divorce, having my
> brother & Dawn (bride to be) living in Saginaw & me having somebody who
> can listen to all my problem. And I just think, and then I start to cry. I try not
> to, but it gets me mad because I think my life is worth nothing.

Just as Craig's thoughts about the next game do not lead to victory, Wendy's
thoughts about "if my parents never got a divorce" and "having my brother &
Dawn (bride to be)," do not ward off her loneliness, tears, and anger.

Realizing that she is not alone, seeing in published writers' narratives
young people who are experiencing problems like her own, Wendy appears to
have found ways of reading and writing—uses for reading and writing, if you
will—that allow her to explore issues of concern to her. Having connected her

literate world with her lived world, as James Boyd White tells us she will, she begins to change them both.[7]

Wendy introduced the changes she was beginning to make with a rhetorical move that asked us to make changes too. With a note "NOT FOR THE CLASS," at the top of some of the writing she composed at this time, she restricted the audience for pieces that explored topics we recognized she had been preparing herself to examine, topics she was not prepared to examine with others. Although Wendy did not wish to share some pieces of her writing with her classmates at this time, she did place those pieces in her portfolio for Jane and me to read.

Teachers who invite students to use reading and writing to explore concerns that preoccupy them in their lives outside of school often find themselves in the position that Jane and I did when Wendy wrote for herself and us about concerns that she was translating into subjects for study, concerns integrally related to the self she was working to compose in her writing. While it goes without saying that we respected the trust Wendy asked of us, that we did not make available to others writings Wendy wished to share only with us, it is worth saying a few words about the issue that Wendy's request and our actions represent because it is an issue that perplexes our profession.

Some educators insist that teachers should not allow students to explore their personal concerns in the talk or writing they do in classrooms, even when students' concerns match those in the reading they are assigned in classrooms. Educators who hold this position argue that teachers whose instructional plans allow students to relate issues that perplex them in personal lives to issues under study in school are invading students' privacy. They claim that by providing opportunities for students to relate personal concerns to school work, teachers are placing themselves in the position of learning things about their students that teachers should not know. Arguing that teachers are not professionally prepared to handle the problems that students might reveal to them, these critics voice an issue that my colleagues and I (and other teachers like us) must address.

I have grappled with this issue across the more than thirty years that I have been a teacher of young people; and I have "worried" it with other teachers, with my students, and with their parents. I hold a position on this issue that I have not reached easily or lightly: Teachers of schoolchildren are never far from the concerns their students bring with them to their studies. If they are, they do not teach students. They may teach subject matter, but they do not teach students.

Linda Brodkey in her important essay "On the Subjects of Class and Gender in 'The Literacy Letters,'"[8] demonstrates powerfully how well-meaning teachers who do not allow students to explore topics of personal concern to them—topics students understand as relating significantly to their school work—disfranchise their students. In her article, Brodkey reproduces an exchange of letters between women enrolled in an adult literacy program and women enrolled in a graduate course in theories and practices of literacy learning. These letters demonstrate how well-meaning "teachers" who do not respond to the issues and themes that "student" writers choose to explore and relate to their school work effectively silence "student" writers. Without meaning to do so, such teachers obstruct students' literacy development.

Nevertheless, the issue is not so easily dismissed. When teachers invite students to make connections between their lived worlds and the work they do in school, teachers place themselves in the position of having to make judgments, not just on the day they decide a particular topic for study or the day they choose a particular text for study, but all day, every day they interact with students. For example, how do teachers respond when students introduce topics or make connections that signal not only students' understandings and misunderstandings of the subject at hand but also sensitive issues in students' lives? In their families' lives? In the lives of their communities?

In some cases—in cases like Wendy's, for example—students' acts of naming and discussing demystify, reconfigure, reapportion, even disspell concerns that have preoccupied them. When this happens, teachers often judge that they need do very little, as Jane and I decided we need do very little when Wendy put words on paper to describe aspects of her lived life that perplexed her. In her acts of composition, Wendy was exploring the meaning of words that had become labels. In her exploration, she was discovering that what she once understood simplistically was in fact most complex. Neither Jane nor I needed to help Wendy in her work. Her writing was a most effective teacher. In our judgment, Wendy needed us to do what we did: to confirm that her work demonstrated she was learning to entertain from multiple perspectives concerns she had once seen from only one perspective; that she was learning to use language to frame, describe, discuss, and resolve issues; that she was learning to read and write by reading and writing to learn.

In other cases (in cases not like Wendy's) teachers' judgments sometimes lead them to undertake more explicit teaching. Teachers often discuss students' writing with them in an effort to help students figure out what is prefigured in their writing. In so doing, teachers often ask students to discuss their writing in terms of questions like these: What is this piece of writing about? Can you tell me more about this section of your writing? Can you write another piece about the same topic/concern/issue? In other words, teachers help students who have been unable to bring their concerns to the level of langauge to find language in which to express those concerns. Teachers do this, of course, because once students have expressed their concerns in language, they may begin a dialogue with those concerns and with the self who composed them.

In still other cases (in cases when students' talk and writing surface issues that not only concern themselves but also concern their teachers for them) teachers' judgments may move them to call on others—parents or professionals with special expertise—to provide students assistance that teachers are not prepared to provide.

When teachers invite students to relate their lived lives to their school studies, some would say they take on potentially difficult work. I would agree, and I would urge that they confront the work of teaching and acknowledge it. If teachers do not allow students to make such sense of their school work as they can in terms of the experiences and images—the prior texts—that students bring to their school work, teachers ensure that those students will not learn in school.

I wish to note here that after Wendy composed the perplexing problems she did not initially wish to share with the classmates in several pieces of writing, then read those pieces of writing herself, and observed her teachers' reactions to them, she was no longer concerned about keeping that writing "private." Still, I have not reproduced those pieces of writing here because they did not figure in the common study of growing-up experiences and the stories people tell about them that Wendy and her classmates conducted together in the *Inquiry and Expression* course. The pieces of Wendy's writing reproduced and discussed here represent the portion of her intellectual work that she contributed to and that figured in the larger study our class conducted collectively.

Wendy's Research Methodology

As Wendy's teachers, at this point in our course, Jane and I kept school. In a mid-year examination, that asked students to compose a series of impromptu essays, we sought to learn how far Wendy and her fellow students had come in *Inquiry and Expression* by testing them in a situation that fits most schoolkeepers' notions of what a test (a writing assessment) should look like. For their examination, we asked students to write about teenage stress in three impromptu essays composed on three different days. On a fourth day, we asked them to revise one of their first three essays or to compose a fourth on the same subject.

Although Wendy told us in her evaluation of our midterm examination that she "hated" the experience "because I don't have a lot of stories to write about plus I hate writing for that long a period," the essays she produced seemed to contradict her words. In reading them and rereading them we understood, however, that they must have been painful to compose. Wendy chose to elaborate on two themes she had been writing about since September: her relationships with her family and her relationships with her peers. In her first two impromptu writings, She wrote about her relationships with her family, more specifically, about her relationship with her mother. She chose to revise her third piece of writing, an essay about her relationships with her peers, on the fourth day of the examination (W-10).

When we compared these three with the four impromptu essays Wendy composed for us in September, we noted her growth as a writer: her improvement in global organization, local control, usage, and the mechanics of writing. We found still more impressive Wendy's continuing exploration of the themes that defined the focus of her intellectual project. "The Most Stressful Situation That I Have Had" (excerpts of which are reproduced here), "Throwing Snowballs From the Roof" (W-9), and "My Friends" (W-10) constitute an obvious invitation, in their themes, situations, and characters, to intertextual readings. We read "The Most Stressful Situation That I Have Had" as a rereading, on our part and Wendy's, of "Unrest at Home" (W-4) and "My Father" (W-5); and we read it as the introduction to another text that Wendy composed in W-9, and W-10.

In "[The Most Stressful Situation That I Have Had]," Wendy recalls:

> The most stressful situation that I have had is when my parents were divorced while I was in the 6th grade. As soon as they were divorced my mother's friend and her two kids moved in with my mom & my brother Steve. It was reallyhard on me and Steve because we wanted our dad to come back to live with us. But it never can true.

And later, Wendy laments:

> When my brother was old enough he joined the Navy. Know he is living with his bride to be. Sometimes when I am upstairs in my bedroom lying down on my waterbed, I just start to think about what had happened with my life. And what would it be like if my parents never got a divorce, having my brother & Dawn (Bride to be) living in Saginaw & me having somebody who can listen to all my problem. And I just think, and then I start to cry. I try not to, but it gets me mad because I think my life is worth nothing.

Reading these passages as a textual extension of W-4 and W-5, we saw Wendy reopen her investigation of her relationship to her parents. Reading these passages as an introduction to a text she composes in them, W-9, and W-10, we saw Wendy reopening her investigation to explore her relationship with her mother. We also saw what were for us signs that Wendy was developing a research method for inquiring into the issues she was studying. In "Unrest at Home" (W-4), after rehearsing the difficulties she was having with relationships in her home, Wendy claimed that she "wanted to live at [her] dads anyway." However, in "My Father" (W-5), after accounting for her parents' divorce, Wendy described an especially painful weekend she spent with her dad, and, in so doing, she problematized the claim she had made in W-4. Moving from a claim about the relationship she wished to have with her dad to a problematization of that claim, Wendy created a crisis in her life with her father, one that required resolution. In W-5, she wrote that her father's drinking "became so bad, that my mom and her friend took my dad into the hospital . . ." where he received treatment for his alcoholism. Having composed a crisis and laid the ground work for its resolution, Wendy inscribed her reconciliation with her father in "the first conversation we evr had," a conversation in which she assures him that she loves him "very much."

In passages from "The Most Stressful Situation I Have Had," W-9, and W-10, following the same research method she used to explore her relationship to her father,[9] Wendy makes claims about her relationship with her mother, problematizes those claims, and frames them into a problem that demands resolution. But she inscribes no resolution to the problem she has framed. In "The Most Stressful Situation That I Have Had," Wendy reopens the text she began in "Unrest at Home" (W-4), supplying her readers more information about the reconfiguration of relationships in her home that occurred when she was in sixth grade. In "Throwing Snowballs From the Roof" (W-9), instead of describing a crisis in her relationship with her mother, Wendy's developing stylistic awareness of her self as a "creative writer" leads her to dramatize that confrontation:

W-9—[Throwing Snowballs From the Roof]

It was in the winter of '86. There was snow on the ground and very cold. me & my friends Tammie & Kurt were over to my house. we were throwing snowballs at cars. All Just out of the blue Kurt asked if we wanted to go up on the roof to throw snowballs. I asked him. What's the hell with you. If I ever was to get caught up there, my mom would kick my ass.

Tammi and Kurt started to call me a chicken Shit. So I got pissed off and we climbed on top of the roof. I was really scared because I was scared to death about heights. We were up there for about 1/2 hour, throwing snowballs at cars. then we jumped down because Tammie & Kurt had to go home.

So I was in the living watching TV when she my mom came home. She was in a pissy ass mood because she was fed up with her job. The next thing I knew. The next door neighbor had told Sandi I was up on the roof and she told my mom. When my mom found out, she went crazy, she started to really bitch me out for being up there. I told her that there was nothing wrong to having some fun. The next thing I knew she started bitching even more. When I looked up to say something, she threw a coffee cup, filled with coffee at the door. The cup shattered into pieces.

I just sat their, then she told me I was grounded for a week and I couldn't have my 16th birthday party. Then she ran out the door. I was never so shocked before in my life. I had never see her act the way she did, but know I understand about all the pressure she was going through.

In W-9, Wendy explicitly expresses her anger toward her mother, anger she suggested in "The Most Stressful Situation That I Have Had," ("It was reallyhard on me and Steve because we wanted our dad to come back to live with us"; "I hated the whole situation"; "I hated Sandi's 1 kid"; "And I just think, and then I start to cry. I try not to, but it gets me mad because I think my life is worth nothing."). With uncharacteristic irony, however, in the first two paragraphs of W-9, Wendy composes a situation that prepares her readers to understand her anger toward her mother as misplaced anger. Not only does she indicate that she is aware of the fact that her actions will displease her mother, but she also indicates that she is frightened by what she is doing:

All Just out of the blue Kurt asked if we wanted to go up on the roof to throw snowballs. I asked him. What's the hell with you. If I ever was to get caught up there, my mom would kick my ass.

> Tammi and Kurt started to call me a chicken Shit. So I got pissed off
> and we climbed on top of the roof. I was really scared because I was scared
> to death about heights.

Although she has disobeyed her mother's expectations and thereby frightened herself, Wendy chooses to be indignant when her mother chastises her for
misbehaving:

> When my mom found out, she went crazy, she started to really bitch me out
> for being up there. I told her that there was nothing wrong to having some
> fun. The next thing I knew she started bitching even more. When I looked up
> to say something, she threw a coffee cup, filled with coffee at the door. The
> cup shattered into pieces

Earlier in the academic year, we recognized several of Wendy's underwritten narrative-essays as curricular invitations she was composing for herself, invitations calling for elaboration and clarification of problems she was working
to define. At this time, we recognized that the dramatic crises she was composing into her narrative-essays were functioning to translate those elaborated and
clarified problems into questions that required answers within Wendy's developing intellectual project.[10] In "My Father" (W-5), for example, we believe Wendy
posed these questions: How can I relate to my father? How shall I relate to him?
And we believe she answered them in this fashion: I can relate to my father after
he undergoes treatment for his illness. I shall relate to him by loving him. We
suspected that Wendy may well have learned this composing strategy for shaping and solving problems from the young-adult novels she was reading in which
action was consistently plotted to rise, climax, fall, and be resolved.

As the students of her texts that we were becoming, we read "My Friends"
(W-10), juxtaposed as it is to "Throwing Snowballs from the Roof" (W-9) as
a move by Wendy to compose a more realistic resolution to the tension between her and her mother than the formulaic one she had been reading and that
she had been composing herself.

W-10—[My Friends]

> There are days when I think to myself, where did I meet my friends at.
> Most of my friends that I hang around with is involved in smoking pot, tak-
> ing speeders and some other kinds of drugs.
>
> I'm the only one out of my friends who has never did any kind of drug
> before in my life. The only think I have ever tried is drinking, but I only
> drink once in a great while. I don't drink beer and all the hard stuff, I drink
> California Coolers.
>
> Most of the time they try to get me to get high or drunk with them. I
> really don't hang around with them too much anymore because I am always
> working, so I guess I use for an excuse.
>
> My best friend Tammie, who has a brain tumor always want to go out
> and party. She gets high and drunk all the time. I don't know why she does
> it, maybe so everybody will thinks she's cool, but drinking and getting high
> is not cool, it is plain stupid.

I thought maybe that by Tammie mixing drugs and alcohol, it ? may have an effect in on the tumor which is lodged in her brain.

While I'm around her & some other friends while they are high, it seems we can communicate a lot better, but while they are straight, all they are concerned about is getting more drugs in the body. I have a problem with being with them while they are high because they want to get into rouble. I mean I have fun with them, but then they get to the point where they want more excitment, so it's hard on me. I usually just tell ? them I have to go home or go to work. Usually my excuses work. All my friends, well most of them any way always ask me why I haven't ever tried drugs. I would just tell them that I can have a great time, just like any other person who is on drugs. The only thing is, is that I am not and never will be for the rest of my life.

Peer pressure is very stressful to a teenager. It has many effects on us, but in many different ways. Your peers may say "if you don't do this or that" it will be the end of a very good relationship between you and your friends. Its hard on me because they think I a I am a total square because I ??t don't do drugs or alcohol. I don't skip school and I get pretty good marks in school. They don't understand what it is like for me. All they are concerned about is getting involve in drugs. They don't even try to understand, and I just wish they would.

In "My Friends," Wendy reflects on her disappointment with her peers in terms that invite her readers to understand W-10, in part, as commentary on "Throwing Snowballs from the Roof." In W-9, when Kurt and Tammie pressure her to join them in throwing snowballs from the roof, Wendy's first reaction to the suggestion is concern about her mother's disapproval. Only secondarily is she concerned about her well-being. Her participation in her friends' scheme earns her what she had anticipated: her mother's anger. It does not cause her harm. In "My Friends," when she writes about the excuses she has developed to avoid getting involved in the "excitement" her friends have continued to propose to her—excitement that carries with it most worrisome consequences—Wendy demonstrates that her mother's concern for her well-being has become her own:

I have a problem with being with them while they are high because they want to get into trouble. I mean I have fun with them, but then they get to the point where they want more excitment, so it's hard on me. I usually just tell them I have to go home or go to work. Usually my excuses work. All my friends, well most of them any way always ask me why I haven't ever tried drugs. I would just tell them that I can have a great time, just like any other person who is on drugs. The only thing is, is that I am not and never will be for the rest of my life.

W-10 offers a significant shift in Wendy's textual persona. She is not the child angry with her parent for disappointments her parent cannot remedy. She is not the child angry with her parent because she wants to break her parent's rules. She is a young woman shaping values and a lifestyle within the circumstances in which she finds herself. The conclusions she composes to W-9 and

W-10 bespeak Wendy's shifting perspective: She concludes W-9 with an observation about her mother: "I understand about all the pressure she was going through"; she concludes W-10 with an observation about her friends: "They don't even try to understand, and I just wish they would."

In the impromptu writings she composed for the midyear examination in *Inquiry and Expression,* Wendy has written her way from childish anger toward more mature understanding. Having offered herself an opportunity to resolve her tension with her mother (as she resolved her tension with her father,) by composing a crisis in their relationship, Wendy takes up her self-composed opportunity differently than she did when she wrote about her father (W-5) and shaped a happy-ever-after resolution to his problems and to her relationship him:

> Ever since he got out of the Hospital, he hasn't touched a drop of alcohol. It has been about a year since he drank. Now all he drinks is pop & coffee. I am so happy that he quit. Now his life is back together & even though he doesn't have my mom, but he does have a son and daughter who loves him very much.

In the trilogy formed of passages from "The Most Stressful Situation That I Have Had," W-9, and W-10, Wendy does not indicate that she feels comfortable or easy with her mother. Rather, she explains that she understands her mother is experiencing unusual pressure. One reading of her understanding is, of course, that the tension between them is her mother's problem and not Wendy's, or not theirs in common. Yet in W-10, Wendy makes a move she has been learning to make in her development as a writer. Although she does not explicitly acknowledge that she may, in part, be responsible for arguments between her mother and her, like the one in W-9, she positions herself in W-10 as an actor in a dramatically realized situation where her friends' values play out against her mother's. Wendy does not say that her mother's indignation is just; she does not claim, as she did with her father, that she loves her mother "very much." Rather, she aligns herself with her mother's values; she positions herself as one who would compose another kind of life from that of her friends. Her statement is implicit, not explicit. Wendy does not say. "There is some righteousness in my mother's indignation"; she does not promise that life is "back together." Her fairy-tale endings are gone, unreplaced at this point in time in her research project.

Wendy's work in "The Most Stressful Situation That I Have Had," W-9, and W-10, along with the work others of our students were doing, led us to plan a program of reading in late January and early February in which we introduced students to a second set of core literary selections. We assigned these selections written about the adolescent experience by two psychologists, a professional educator, and a sociologist because we wanted to give students the opportunity to read complex texts from their hard-earned perspective as experts on the subject of growing up—a reading experience most of our students had not previously had. We wanted to initiate discussions of the common themes in our students' inquiries into growing up.[11]

We compiled and distributed a course pack of the readings we had selected and invited students to engage in dialogues with the writers of the selections. In marginal notes, we encouraged students to ask questions of the authors whose pieces they were reading just as they asked questions of us and each other when they read the writing we were composing during our course of study together. Students wrote informal responses to the essays they were reading, and we discussed the essays and their responses in class. An excerpt from the response Wendy composed to "Commonality," a chapter from Theodore Sizer's *Horace's Compromise,* illustrates the dialogues she was having with texts. It illustrates not only her comprehension of Sizer's text, but also the purposefulness of her reading and its critical quality. Wendy is clearly reading at this time to learn more about the issues she is interrogating within her own intellectual project:

> . . . I agree on the part where young people are pressured by their friends to have sex. Even when they really don't want to. They think being a virgin is like a festering appendix. The kids today want to experience in what adults do. Like haveing sex, &drinking, just to be an adult. They want to grow up faster. Why can't the kids, (teenagers) just have fun while they can. I can't see a kid who is 12 years old get pregnant & then go on & have the baby. When she is just a kid her self. Now she has a child of her own, she is pressured into acting as a adult and being a parent. I agree that the sexual relations from the 1960's to now 1988 has changed dramitically. Most women waited until being a wife. I you did get pregnant they made you feel wrong doing they ignore you, kick you out of school. Now in 1988 if you are a teenager and you get pregnant it still is almost the same feeling but most schools would not kick you out. I disagree on the part of a white lade getting pregnant by a black man would be banished from the community just because of the color of their skin. If they truly love each other there is nothing wrong with it. I can't believe that "almost ½ of all sixteen year old boys & ⅓ of girls had sexual intercourse. I don't see how just kids can have sex. If the girl get pregnant & she can raise the baby work to feed the baby & study for college. Why don't they think about what can happen. It could change their lives forever. Some maybe for the good, but they probably look back to see what they missed & some for the bad. Not going to college for further education, wedlocks & not really loving each other.

By February in the *Inquiry and Expression* course, Wendy had not only developed as a researcher, writer, and reader, but she had also developed an awareness of herself as researcher, as writer, and as reader.

Wendy Publishes Her Research

In February, after the midyear examination, when they shifted their focus from collecting and composing growing-up stories to critiquing and analyzing those stories in light of their readings in social science literature, students in the *In-*

quiry and Expression course decided to compose and publish an anthology of writings that would represent their own growing-up experiences in Saginaw in the 1970s and the 1980s. In preparation for this work, students read a collection of seven pieces of each other's writing. In small groups and as a class, they discussed their literature. After students became fully familiar with the range of themes and literary styles that characterized each other's growing-up experiences and stories and advised each other about which pieces of their writing were most successful and why, Wendy chose to develop "Going Up North" (W-7) for publication. In her choice of an essay, she elected to inscribe the good times she and her family had together when they were traveling in "Camping in Tawas City" (W-11):

W-11—Camping in Tawas City

When I was little, about four or five, my family and I went up north a lot. We belonged to a camping club called the "Timbertown Travelers." Timbertown is what people called Saginaw back then. We would go camping almost every weekend during the summertime. There were about ten families in the group all together. We had a great time when we went up north. We would have potluck dinners and go trick or treating to all of the trailers on Halloween.

I remember one cold day in January, when we went to Tawas City on a camping trip. Our family and the Martin family hung out with each other. The Martins had a boy, Mike, and two girls, Rhonda and Kim. After we got settled down, my brother Steve and I went over to get Mike, Rhonda, and Kim, so that we could all go and get something to eat. We left their trailer and, because it was a long walk, we decided to jump the fence to go to the A&W restaurant. When we walked in, everybody in the restaurant just stared at us. We couldn't figure out why, so we kept on walking until we found an empty booth to sit down. After we finished eating, Rhonda leaned over to me and said, "Put that mug under your hat."

I said, "Are you nuts? I'm not gonna get caught stealing a mug."

"Oh, come on, she whined. "You're not gonna get caught. Who'll know?"

"Well, if you want it that bad, you steal it."

"No, sause I don't have a hat and you do. Besides, they will get suspicious if I wear your hat."

"O.k., but if I get caught, it's your fault."

I thought maybe something was wrong with my brain for stealing a stupid mug worth pennies. I quickly put the mug under my hat, and we left very swiftly and sneakily. Then, as soon as we were out the door, I found myself running with the mug in my hand. When we got to the trailer entrance, we had to jump the fence to get back into the trailer park.

We went back into the trailer and quickly shut the door. We all sat down and started to laugh, because we didn't get caught. After we stopped laughing, we decided to play a fast game called "Spoons". After we played for a while, Mike got bored and decided to go ice fishing at a pond outside of the park. When Mike walked out the door, my brother Steve decided to go with him. After they both left, and Kim, Rhonda, and I decided to sneak up on them.

When Mike and Steve got to the pond, Mike was the first one on the ice. We were hiding by the bushes when we heard something. The next thing we knew, Mike had fallen into the water. We ran from the bushes where Steve was watching him. When we got to the edge of the pond, Kim tried a rescue attempt on Mike, but when she started to make the attempt to rescue him, Mike just stood up in the middle of the pond, drenched with icy water. He said that the water only came to his knees. We burst out laughing. We all helped Mike out of the water and then hurried up to get back to the trailer so Mike could change his clothes.

We all took an oath, vowing we would never tell our parents, because they would kill us for not telling them what had all happened that weekend in Tawas City. But I'm hoping when they read this story they will forgive us. When we look back, we will remember the great times we had with the Timbertown Travelers' Club.

In "Camping in Tawas City" (W-11) we read several things we were not surprised to find in light of Wendy's developing work. We read a text in which Wendy refined the first sustained dramatic action she had composed by replacing indirect speech in the restaurant scene with direct dialogue that she worked purposefully to learn to compose. She revises this passage in (W-7):

> After we got finished eating, Rhonda told me to put an A & W rootbeer mug under my hat. When I asked her why, "she said, She wanted to take home." I told her that I wasn't gonna do it, because I didn't want to get busted. She said that I wouldn't. I told her that something was wrong with her brain. I thought that the cold had something to do with it, but I finally gave in.

into this passage in (W-11):

> After we finished eating, Rhonda leaned over to me and said, "Put that mug under your hat."
> I said, "Are you nuts? I'm not gonna get caught stealing a mug."
> "Oh, come on, she whined. "You're not gonna get caught. Who'll know?"
> "Well, if you want it that bad, you steal it."
> "No, cause I don't have a hat and you do. Besides, they will get suspicious if I wear your hat."
> "O.k., but if I get caught, it's your fault."
> I thought maybe something was wrong with my brain for stealing a stupid mug worth pennies.

In her revision of "Going Up North," Wendy has made small but significant changes. In the W-7 version, she is the pawn in Rhonda's plan. Wendy writes: "I told her there was something wrong with her brain." But in W-11, Wendy recognizes herself as the actor in the scene: "I thought maybe something was wrong with my brain for stealing a stupid mug worth pennies." We read this revision, as well as another small but significant one that Wendy composes to close W-11, as indications of her developing understanding that she is responsible for her actions, that her life is not determined simply by the actions of others. Wendy concluded W-7 with this passage:

We all took an oath saying we would never tell our parents, because they would kill us. Till this day, the still have no idea what all had happen that weekend, and probaby never will. When we look back, we will remember the great times we had with the Timbertown Camping Club.

In W-11, she revised that conclusion to read this way:

We all took an oath, vowing we would never tell our parents, because they would kill us for not telling them what had all happened that weekend in Tawas City. But I'm hoping when they read this story they will forgive us. When we look back, we will remember the great times we had with the Timbertown Travelers' Club.

When she wrote W-7, Wendy moved herself and her parents back to earlier happier times. In writing for *The Bridge*, she chose to inscribe and publish those times. But in W-11, Wendy does not want to leave her family in those earlier times before their troubles. She moves them into a time after those troubles, when she can acknowledge that each of us makes mistakes for which we need to be forgiven.

Assessing Wendy's Learning

[W]hat is called for in our life with language, and with each other, is
an art of composition for which my name is "intellectual integration":
the heart of it lies in making texts (and communities) in which place
is given not merely to one, but to a variety of languages and voices.

White, 1990, xiv.

Jane, Jay, Sharon, and I would argue that our students' literacy should be measured by their uses of reading and writing to realize the meaningful, communicative discourse that constituted the dialogic curriculum of the *Inquiry and Expression* course. For us, the work students and teachers did together to develop and publish *The Bridge*—the product of a mutually realized curriculum—offers us the most meaningful information we can gather about students' potential abilities to use reading and writing in the world. But ours are lonely voices in the discussions about the assessment of reading and writing underway in our country today.[12] To provide evidence of our students' learning to others who are not convinced that their published writing is a valid measure of our students' reading and writing competencies, we constructed a final examination in writing that asked students to compose texts on their own, without advice or consultation.

We decided to ask students to write for two days at the end of May about the Montague Inn, a gracious bed and breakfast in Saginaw. We saw this writing task not only as an occasion for a final examination, but also as an opportunity to finish some unfinished business. In March, we had visited the inn on a field trip. Because we were busy in class at the time with our work to publish *The Bridge,* we had not discussed the inn and our trip to it as fully as we wished.[13] For their final examination, we invited Wendy and her classmates to refer to their memories of their visit to the inn, the notes they had taken during that visit, and the pieces of writing they had read about the inn to prepare themselves to write about the inn during two class sessions. We encouraged students to draft an essay on the first day of the exam and revise it on the second day. At the beginning of the first day, Wendy composed W-12; mid-way through the 55-minute class period, she put it aside and composed W-13. In the reproductions of these pieces below, Sections of the compositions that Wendy crossed out after she wrote them are italicized:

W-12—The Wedding

May, 1988

It's 9:00 a.m. Saturday morning and my mother, Dawn, and I were getting ready for Dawn and Steve's wedding. We were in our bedroom in the Montague Inn waiting until 1:00 p.m. when the wedding is supposed to start I don't remember too much about how it all got started, but I'll try to fill you in on how they wanted their wedding at the Montague Inn.

I think it all started when my brother Steve flew down to Saginaw to get everything ready for their wedding which will take place June 11.

Steve was staying with us, while Dawn had to stay in Florida to work. While Steve was home, he asked me to go visit my dad, so I told him I would. We were driving to my dad's house and we were passing the Montague Inn. Steve asked me what that place was and I told him it was a house that people could have weddings and where people could stay overnight while maybe on a business trip or even while on vacation.

W-13—Montague Inn

The Wedding

May

It's 9:00 a.m. Saturday morning, and my mother, Dawn, and I were getting ready for my brother Steve and Dawn's wedding. We were in our bedroom at the Montague Inn, waiting until 1:00 p.m. when the wedding is supposed to start. I don't remember too much about how it all got started, but I'll try to fill you in how they wanted there wedding there. I think it all started when my brother went on a trip to Michigan for the Armed Forces. He was staying with my mom and I, while Dawn was getting all the wedding plans worked out while in Florida. My brother and I were driving to my dad's house and on the way there we passed the Montague Inn. Steve asked me what that place was and I told him that it was a house that people could have weddings and where people could stay while maybe on a business trip or while on vacation. He couldn't believe it when I told him that weddings were actually held there in the *Herb Garden* in the backyard by the river.

Then Steve came up with the idea to have their wedding there. I thought it was a great idea. Then he asked me to find out some information from there, so I did. I found out a lot of stuff. I wasn't sure if he wanted to know what I found out because I thought he might say it wasn't important. I finally told him what I found out. *That it was an old home before Mr. and Mrs.*

Kinney bought it and remodled it. And that plenty of weddings have taken place there and all of them turned out great. So when Steve had to fly back to Florida, he told Dawn all about his idea of having there wedding at the Montague Inn. She loved it. They called that night to make all the arrangements for their wedding. Everything was set. All they had to do was to show up on there wedding day which was June 11, the day after my graduation. Well after I had graduated we (my mother, Dawn and I) spent the night there to get ready for the wedding. Steve and my dad stayed in the room next door. I told him that I found out that a couple named Mr. and Mrs. Kinney bought the house and remodeled it. It became a beautiful home with plenty of rooms where people can stay. The Montague Inn is one of a kind. Friends of the Kinney's had helped out in the remodeling and had plenty of fun. I told Steve I also found out that the Inn was a very popular place because of its nice faculties and the way they treat you like one of the family.

Every thing was going along great. I was now getting closer to 1:00 and everybody was getting nervous. I went walking around and I noticed that there were a lot of bedroom and even a kitchen downstairs. I was so amused that I just kept walking around admiring all the beautiful things. I even lost track of time. When I finally noticed what time it was I only had 10 minutes until the wedding started. I ran to the bedroom and got dressed. Then it was time. We went out to the Herb Garden where everything was set up beautifully. Then the wedding bells began to ring. The wedding was starting. I couldn't believe it. I was actually getting a sister-in-law. Then it happened! They were married. I was so happy. Now that the wedding was over, now I could look forward to the reception. That was held in the hall. It was a great reception. There was dancing and music and everybody was having a great time. Then Steve and Dawn left for there honeymoon in Hawaii. Steve and Dawn were married June 11, 1988 at the Montague Inn. Now they live in Jacksonville, Florida with one son Steve Jr. and one daughter named Lisa

Given the kind of writings they were—composed within one 55-minute class period—and the time when they were written—at the end of our course of study together—we could not help but compare the hastily composed W-12 and W-13 with W-1, W-2, W-3, and W-4, the first writings Wendy submitted to us in *Inquiry and Expression*. Peppered with mechanical and usage errors that characterize her unrevised writing, the compositions Wendy composed during the first day of her final exam in May not only provide us a picture of the quality of her untutored writing at the time, but also create a picture of the workings of the dialogic curriculum. In W-12 and W-13, Wendy creates an occasion that enables her to fulfill her teachers' plans for her to write about the Montague Inn and to pursue her own project of composing the relationships between and among the members of her family. Circling back to her earlier texts, in a series of drafts and revisions, she gathers the characters that matter to her—her mother, her father, her brother Steve, and his fiance Dawn:

It's 9:00 a.m. Saturday morning and my mother, Dawn, and I were getting ready for Dawn and Steve's wedding. We were in our bedroom in the Montague Inn waiting until 1:00 p.m. when the wedding is supposed to start (W-13).

Well after I had graduated we (my mother, Dawn and I) spent the night there
to get ready for the wedding. Steve and my dad stayed in the room next door
(W-14).

And she brings them to the Montague Inn, which she describes in some detail
both to create a setting for the wedding and to satisfy her teachers' plan that
she write about the inn in this final exam:

> I told him that I found out that a couple named Mr. and Mrs. Kinney
> bought the house and remodeled it. It became a beautiful home with plenty
> of rooms where people can stay. The Montague Inn is one of a kind. Friends
> of the Kinney's had helped out in the remodeling and had plenty of fun. I
> told Steve I also found out that the Inn was a very popular place because of
> its nice faculties and the way they treat you like one of the family.
>   Every thing was going along great. I was now getting closer to 1:00 and
> everybody was getting nervous. I went walking around and I noticed that there
> were a lot of bedroom and even a kitchen downstairs. I was so amused that I
> just kept walking around admiring all the beautiful things. I even lost track of
> time. When I finally noticed what time it was I only had 10 minutes until the
> wedding started. I ran to the bedroom and got dressed. Then it was time. We
> went out to the Herb Garden where everything was set up beautifully (W-14).

Characters gathered, setting described, Wendy stages a fairy-tale wedding,
like the ones she has encountered in the young-adult novels she was reading:

> Then it was time. We went out to the Herb Garden where everything was set
> up beautifully. Then the wedding bells began to ring. The wedding was start-
> ing. I couldn't believe it. I was actually getting a sister-in-law. Then it hap-
> pened! They were married. I was so happy. Now that the wedding was over,
> now I could look forward to the reception. That was held in the hall. It was a
> great reception. There was dancing and music and everybody was having a
> great time. Then Steve and Dawn left for there honeymoon in Hawaii. Steve
> and Dawn were married June 11, 1988 at the Montague Inn. Now they live
> in Jacksonville, Florida with one son Steve Jr. and one daughter named Lisa
> (M-14).

Although we encouraged students to revise the compositions they had
written the previous day, on the second day of their final examination, Wendy
chose not to do that. She completely abandoned the work she had begun in W-
12 and W-13, electing instead to leave the fairy tale she had been composing
behind her. In W-14, a piece we described to each other as realistic fiction,
Wendy wrote her final composition for *Inquiry and Expression*.

W-14—The Montague Inn

> I remember growing up in Florida with my mother in a small apartment with
> only one bedroom and one bathroom and the dining room connected with
> each other. I would always dream about living in a huge house, having at
> least ten bedrooms and at least four bathrooms. I knew that someday I would

either be able to live in a house that big or I could one day see the inside of one. I remember the day my mother told me we were going to visit my mother's sister in Saginaw, Michigan. I was so excited, I wanted to leave right away. My mother told me we were leaving the next day, so I hurried up and packed everything that I could. When we got to the Detroit Metropolitan Airport, my mother's sister Pat was waiting for us to get off the plane. When we were in the airport we saw my Aunt Pat waiting for us. I just dropped my bags and ran over to her to give her a big hug. On the way home my Aunt Pat told us what she had in mind for us to do while we stayed with Aunt Pat and her family. She said the most exciting thing to do is to see the Montague Inn. I had asked her what it was and she told me that it was an old house where people from anywhere could stay the night. My Aunt Pat told my mother and I that the home had about 15 bedrooms. I was so excited that I could finally see a beautiful home like that I asked her when we could go see it and she did the following day because we had to go back to her house so we could rest and get something to eat.

After we had something to eat I went to bed because I thought that the night would go faster. But it took me a while to fall alseep because I was so excited. Then the day came to visit the Montague Inn. When we got there I was astonished at such a wonderful home it was. I couldn't imagine anything bigger. When we walked in the doors I could feel a chill running up my spine. Mr. and Mrs. Kinney gave us a four of the home and told us how her and her husband and friends did most of the remodeling themselves. They told us about Mr. Montague and his two children. They showed us all the bedrooms and the outside by the herb garden. It was great. After the tour was over Mr. and Mrs. Kinney told us how nice of a pleasure it was to show us around. We thanked her and as we were going out the door my Aunt Pat remembered that she had locked her keys in her car. So my Aunt had to call her house and have her son Todd bring out an extra pair. While we waited, Mr. and Mrs. Kinney asked us to stay for lunch. So we did. The lunch was really too fancy for me though, I just assume stick with my 2 favorites Old Town Drive Inn and Macdonald's. Todd had arrived just as we finished eating. We thanked her again and left. When my mother and I left for Florida I said to myself that someday I would start a Montague Inn where I live.

In fulfillment of our plans and her project, Wendy writes about the Montague Inn and her family. And she does something else: Wendy's last piece of writing for the *Inquiry and Expression* course looked to us as if in it she had composed another curricular invitation to herself. With W-14, she appears to have concluded the text she was writing during the 1987–1988 academic year and to have introduced a new one that does not focus on the past, but rather looks to the future.

I smiled when I first read the last piece of writing Wendy composed for the course we had constructed together, and I smile again as I read it now. Perhaps I do so because she begins the piece by placing herself in Florida, a place I know she likes because she told me so in one of the earliest texts she composed for our course (W-3). Perhaps I do so because because I enjoy the way she moves herself from Florida to the Montague Inn, which she has to write about to fulfill her teachers' plans for this assignment. Perhaps I do so because she mentions my friends, Kathryn and Norman Kinney, innkeepers of the Montague Inn, my home away from home when I was in Saginaw. Perhaps I do so because she writes about misplaced cars keys, and that detail makes me remember that Wendy misplaced her car keys the day our class visited the Montague Inn. Perhaps I do so because Wendy leaves the inn to take a journey with her mother, and I am a mother. Perhaps I smile for some combination of these reasons; perhaps for all of them. I know I smile because the text makes connections with me and for me.

In his book *Justice as Translation*, James Boyd White argues that "what is called for in our life with language, and with one another, is an art of composition," a capacity for "intellectual integration" (xiv). White explains what he means by this "art of composition," this capacity for "intellectual integration" in this way:

> [W]hat I mean by integration is a kind of composition, and that in a literal, and literary sense: a putting together of two things to make out of them a third, a new whole, with a meaning of its own. In this process the elements combined do not lose their identities but retain them, often in clarified form; yet each comes to mean something different as well, when it is seen in relation to the other. In this sense each element is transformed, as it becomes part of something else, an entity existing at a new level of complexity. At the same time we ourselves are transformed as well, both as makers of the new object in the world and as those who engage with it (p. 4).

In W-14, Wendy's final piece of writing for the *Inquiry and Expression* course, I observed an act of "intellectual integration" of the kind that White describes. In this piece, Wendy composes two things—the people and events that have defined her lived life and the texts that have constituted her research project—into a third thing—a world that she can make, that she can inhabit in the future, that her past experiences inform but do not delineate, that her research project posits but does not assure. In her composition, Wendy combines elements from her lived world and her studies; she does not change their identities, but retains them in clarified form. In her act of composition, Wendy's past experiences and her studies each come to mean something different in the light of one another. In this sense, each is transformed, becoming something else, existing at a new level of complexity. And, I would argue, Wendy becomes someone else, someone able to live in the world she imagines in W-14—should she choose to do so. For herself, Wendy has composed "possible worlds."

Because I share James Boyd White's belief "that what is called for in our life with language, and with one another, is an art of composition," and because I believe that individuals' ability to evaluate experience in the light of texts and texts in the light of experience is perhaps the most valid measure of learning, when I looked for evidence of the learning of students in the *Inquiry and Expression* course, I looked at their ability to integrate the existential and textual realms of their experience in their compositions. In Wendy's work and in our other students' work, I found such evidence.

The End in View

I have composed the first two chapters of this book so that they would unwind like clips of "home movies," documenting the same unfolding drama from two angles. Focusing my cameras on particular actors, I hoped to encourage readers to imagine the students and teachers who worked together in aging school buildings in a rust belt city. By editing, titling, and subtitling footage and occasionally freezing the frame, I've highlighted several story lines playing out in my film, and I've emphasized my reading of events. Finally, to illustrate the two kinds of dialogues that I claim to be constitutive of a dialogic curriculum—dialogues between and among teachers and students and dialogues students conduct with themselves—I have dubbed voices over the pictures I have provided. I have done these things to argue for a conception of and a conviction about curriculum.

In my view, curricula developed in schoolrooms—especially curricula developed for the study of language, literacy, and literature—must allow teachers and students to assume more responsibility for their development than is customarily the case. Like everyone else, I want teachers and students to assume responsibility for the outcomes of their teaching and learning. I am persuaded that teachers' and students' co-construction of curricula—curricula that teachers introduce with topical questions; curricula that students address in terms of the images, language, and logic of their home communities; curricula that teachers and students co-compose in reciprocally realized interactions within (inter)discipline-based studies; curricula that students transport into their home communities in the form of meaningful and purposeful products of their learning—is the most promising way to achieve this end.

I argue for my conception of curriculum and my convictions about it with an end in view. I imagine a society in which classrooms and the lessons that unfold within them acknowledge the images, language, logic, and experience that students bring to school. I imagine a society in which classrooms and the curricula that unfold within them enable all learners to extend and enrich the understandings they bring with them to school for their own and the common good. I imagine a democratic society in which people speak and listen to one another and teach and learn from one another for the benefit of us all. In the society I imagine, dialogue will abound and learning will flourish.

Notes

1. Because I spent only two days each week in Saginaw, Jane, Sharon, our students, and I wrote letters and electronic mail to one another when I was in Ann Arbor.

2. In part we developed interpretative case studies of our students' literacy learning

to address a concern we share with another teacher-researcher. In his essay, "Writing in a Philosophy Class," in *Research in the Teaching of English.* 20:3 (October 1986): 225–262, Stephen M. North indicates this concern:

> One of the peculiarities of composition research's treatment of student writing has been that, despite an otherwise voracious methodological eclecticism, it has never adopted any hermeneutical method: that is, a method wherein the primary concern is to interpret the writing of individual students as meaningful, communicative discourse (228).

3. Because many of our students were parents of infant children, almost all held full-time jobs outside of school, and some were both parents and workers, we promised that the work we would require of them could be completed during class time. Many students elected to do work for the course outside of classtime. In fact, a majority of them came to school on Saturdays in the spring when we were working to publish *The Bridge,* but we did not require them to do so. Any time they spent working for the course outside of school was time they chose to invest in it.

4. At the same time that she was drafting, revising, and editing three growing-up stories, Wendy was reading a number of young adult novels written about the themes she was exploring in her own writing.

5. See Jerome Bruner. *Actual Minds, Possible Worlds.* (Cambridge, MA: Harvard University Press, 1986):25.

6. To fulfill course assignments, Wendy composed reviews of Nora Sterling's *You Would If You Loved Me* (New York: Avon, 1982); Todd Strassner's *Angel Dust Blues* (New York: Putnam, 1979); and Tommy Hallowell's *Varsity Coach* (New York: Bantam, 1986).

7. In his important book, *When Words Lose Their Meaning.* (Chicago: The University of Chicago Press, 1984), James Boyd White writes:

> Writing is never merely the transfer of information, whether factual or conceptual, from one mind to another, as much as our talk about it assumes, but is always a way of acting both upon the language, which the writer perpetually reconstitutes in his use of it, and upon the reader (6).

8. Linda Brodkey, "On the Subjects of Class and Gender in "The Literacy Letters,'" *College English* 51:2 (February, 1989):125–41.

9. I believe that the mid-year examination in *Inquiry and Expression* may have had something to do with Wendy's decision to write about her relationship to her mother. We teachers had decided that we would each tell a stressful story about our own teenage years to illustrate the kinds of stories students might write for their exams. At the beginning of each of the four days of the exam, one of us told or read a story about ourselves, a narrative within which we intentionally reflected on the events we reported. Jane told her story the first day of the exam in Wendy's class. The story made Jane vulnerable to her students, who, like Wendy, clearly respected her and were fond of her. I believe Jane's willingness to share and reflect on a sensitive problem she experienced as a teenager invited our students to do the same.

10. See "My Father" (W-5), "Tammie" (W-6), "Going Up North" (W-7), and *Varsity Coach* (W-8).

11. We asked students to read "Paths to Adulthood," the first chapter of *Being Adolescent: Conflict and Growth in the Teenage Years* (New York: Basic Books, 1984), written by two psychologists from The University of Chicago, Mihaly Csikszentmihalyi and Reed Larson; "Commonality," the third chapter of Theodore Sizer's well-known critiques of public education in the United States, *Horace's Compromise* (Boston: Houghton Mifflin Co., 1984); and Joshua Meyrowitz's "The Adultlike Child and the Childlike Adult: Socialization in an Electronic Age," an essay published in *Daedalus: The Journal of the American Academy of Arts and Sciences* (Summer, 1984):19–48.

12. With reference to Wendy Gunlock's writings, this argument is made in some detail in Patricia Lambert Stock, "The Rhetoric of Writing Assessment," in Vito Perrone Ed., *Expanding Student Assessment: The 1991 ASCD Yearbook.* (Washington, DC: ASCD, 1991):72–105.

13. We had left the experience of visiting the Montague Inn largely unstudied. One day in class, we composed thank you notes to Kathryn Kinney, one of the inn's owners, who had given us a tour of it and told us stories about the original owners of the house. We also wrote to members of the inn's staff, who had described to us both the renovations they had undertaken to convert the historic house into an inn and the nature of their work to operate the inn on a day-to-day basis. Another day in class, we read several pieces of writing composed about the inn—a press release for its opening and compositions written by community college students who also had toured it.

3

Teacher Research as Storytelling

I will tell you something about stories,
[he said]
They aren't just entertainment.
Don't be fooled.
They are all we have you see,
all we have to fight off
illness and death.

You don't have anything
if you don't have stories.

Leslie Marmon Silko, Ceremony, 1977, 2

Loren Barritt, a professor of curriculum and instruction in the School of Education in The University of Michigan, is fond of saying: "Research is just the story someone tells. What counts is who gets to tell the story."

In this statement, Barritt means, of course, to question both the forms in which research in education are conducted and presented in the United States today and the roles and relationships that exist among professional educators. Research is not usually thought of as storytelling, and teachers who conduct and present their inquiries in the form of stories are not usually thought of as researchers.

By way of accounting for the research I conducted as a teacher in the *Inquiry and Expression* course, the manner in which I have presented it in this book, and the claims I have and will make for it, in this chapter I do three things. First, I indicate why the research that teachers do goes largely unrecognized; second, I offer an explanation about why teachers conduct and present their research in the form of storytelling; and finally I argue that teachers' stories contain insights into teaching and learning that are not found elsewhere, that teachers' research, conducted in reflective storytelling, provides our field a body of knowledge with potential to influence teaching and learning—beneficially.

The Customary Conduct
of Research in Education

Like Donald Schon in his important book, *The Reflective Practitioner,* Loren Barritt draws critical attention to the predominant model of the professional practice of education in our society today, one that defines both the roles and relationships of professional educators in terms of positivism. This doctrine developed in the nineteenth century accounts for both the rise of science and technology and the parallel "social movement aimed at applying the achievements of science and technology to the well-being of mankind [sic]."[1] Donald Schon explains that within this model:

> [R]esearch is institutionally separate from practice, connected to it by carefully defined relationships of exchange. Researchers are supposed to provide the basic and applied science from which to derive techniques for diagnosing and solving the problems of practice. Practitioners are supposed to furnish researchers with problems for study and with tests of the utility of research results. The researcher's role is distinct from, and usually considered superior to, the role of the practitioner.[2]

Despite the fact that positivism is long since dead in theory, the roles and relationships it has constituted in the practice professions are still firmly in place. Teachers rarely get to tell their versions of the story of teaching and learning, and when they do, they do not usually report their insights in terms that are generally recognized as contributing to the knowledge base that informs practice in education. When individuals inside or outside the profession of education say: "The research shows . . . ," they are not usually indicating research conducted and reported by teachers in terms that teachers find meaningful.

Although critical theory has argued persuasively against this distinction of roles and responsibilities, work to integrate practice and research in the profession of education in a theoretically sound fashion has been slow to develop. The teaching and research I report in this book represent my effort to integrate teaching practice and educational research in a theoretically sound fashion and thereby to create a theory that has some promise of contributing beneficially to both the practice of teaching and the conduct of research in my profession.

The Conduct of Teacher Research

My effort takes shape within a developing body of praxis-oriented research being developed by educators who refer to themselves as teacher-researchers because they wish to emphasize the fact that they conduct their research into teaching and learning phenomenologically: by observing, reflecting on, and making claims about phenomena from the perspective of individuals living with and through them. During the last ten years, particularly among teachers of literacy, a growing number of praxis-oriented teacher-researchers, in schools, colleges, and universities have been conducting inquiries into teaching and learning for the purpose of informing our practice and contributing beneficially to the knowledge base a growing number of our colleagues are turning to to inform their practice.[3]

One of the reasons that teachers' research has not been taken as seriously as I would argue it should be is that teachers customarily conduct and report research in anecdotal forms—in the fashion in which Jane, Jay, Sharon, and I conducted our research to develop instruction in the *Inquiry and Expression* course, in the fashion in which I report my research in the first two chapters of this book.

That teachers tell anecdotes when discussing teaching is common knowledge. What is not generally recognized are the functions that shaping, reshaping, and rehearsing of anecdotes play in the research we informally and—I would claim—systematically conduct into our practice. For example, when Jane and I began to shape the anecdote about Gilbert's mother's growing-up story, we gathered pertinent information about a teaching-learning interaction. We collected data, if you will. When we reshaped the anecdote for colleagues, first in one setting, then in another, we selected, deleted, organized, and analyzed the information we had gathered for a particular purpose: to effect better teaching and learning. The anecdotes we teacher-researchers tell and account for to one another function in our research community as what Kenneth Burke calls representative anecdotes: "summations, containing implicitly what the system that is developed from [them] contains explicitly."[4]

In our professional talk, we teachers allude to the library of anecdotes we share. For example, should we wish to bring to bear in another discussion the generative understandings, guiding principles, and working theories we have developed as a result of our study of the events surrounding Gilbert's mother's growing-up story, we are not likely to do so by claiming that: "When students take risks that make them and their families vulnerable to misinterpretation or worse, those students prepare themselves and their classmates to learn." We are more likely to do so by invoking an anecdote: "Remember the time when Gilbert played the tape of his mother's growing-up story."

Teachers avoid abstract theoretical statements when we talk with each other about our professional work because while such statements may be informative, they are not representative of teaching and learning. Anecdotal accounts, populated and overpopulated as they are with meaning and significance, seem to serve us more usefully as we research the dynamic interactions that constitute teaching and learning in our classrooms. Sometimes we begin by testing the dimensions of an anecdote one of us has told the others: Telling and retelling it, we place and replace it in contexts that enrich its meaning. As we add and subtract details, we translate the anecdote into an event, a significant occurrence within one of the larger narratives that define our teaching practice.[5] Other times we surround an anecdote with analogous ones ("That reminds me of the time when . . ."). In such cases, the trajectory of our anecdotes charts the course of our research. We compare, contrast, sort, elaborate, and refine our anecdotes until we have identified the elements that name the family resemblances in them.

All the while, of course, we interpret and reinterpret them in the light of the larger narratives that shape our professional practice. Situating specific teaching-learning moments in the material circumstances in which they occur and reflecting on them in their own terms, rather than in another, specialized discourse, we replay them, inviting colleagues who have not experienced those moments with us to examine them with us as we re-search them. As we freeze the frame on particular interactions, such as the one that occurred when Gilbert shared his mother's growing-up story, we make a move that our fellow teacher-researchers recognize. Drawing attention to them, we present our colleagues with problems for study. In so doing, we invite members of our research community to reach into their memories for analogous teaching-learning moments that have occurred in their classrooms and, in light of those moments, to join us in making sense of them so that we may improve our teaching practice.

When we are unable to translate our anecdotes into events that have meaning and significance within the underlying plots and themes on which we rely to account for our experience, we become aware of some fault line in our larger narratives. The teacher-research movement itself can be described as one response to the failure of the "objectivist" narrative that developed within the social sciences to speak so prevented much guided educational research from meaningfully and purposefully to education's teaching practitioners.

Teacher talk has too often been denigrated as just one social manifestation of gossip: teachers' lounge prattle, post-class complaining, recitals of old stories. Teacher research is too often brushed aside as merely anecdotal: robbed of value because it is occasional and rooted in occasions; not worth notice because of its particularity. My argument for teacher talk, for the power of anecdote, for the importance of narrative in educational research rests in just these characteristics: in their very occasionality, in their very particularity. Teachers who read the anecdote that Jane and I shared with our colleagues as significant recognize elements of the anecdote as similar to ones they have experienced. In the particularities in the anecdote, they recognize particularities in the circumstances in which they teach. Furthermore, when teachers respond to telling anecdotes, we do so as good readers. We read the particularities in the telling against the particularities we would tell, looking for new ways to respond and act in analogous situations, on analogous occasions. As good readers do, we respond aesthetically to figured shapes of human activity that enrich our sensibilities. As we work to enrich our sensibilities and our understandings, they work to enrich our practice.

Theorists of teacher research are not alone in arguing for the value of narrative—anecdote and storytelling—as uniquely appropriate methods for improving practice and constructing knowledge in their professions. For example, in her book *Doctors' Stories: The Narrative Structure of Medical Knowledge*, Kathryn Montgomery Hunter, Professor of Medicine and Codirector of the Ethics and Human Values in Medicine Program in Northwestern University Medical School, describes how doctors tell and retell stories not only to diagnose their patients' illnesses and to teach one another how best to care for patients but also to enrich and extend medicine's knowledge base.[6] In a chapter she entitles "'There Was This One Guy . . .': Anecdotes in Medicine," Hunter claims that because doctors tell anecdotes about anomalous cases, about illnesses that fail to fit currently held understandings of disease, anecdotes play an important function in the advancement of medical knowledge and practice.[7]

Elaborating on the function of anecdotes in the building of knowledge in medicine, she writes:

> Anecdotes serve as critical commentary on such things as the published criteria for a diagnosis or for the stages of a disease. They are useful not only in locating research problems but also in keeping alive a skepticism about new knowledge claims in a hierarchical, authoritarian discipline. As rough accounts of unexpected and occasionally the improbable, they are frequently the as-yet-unorganized evidence at the forefront of clinical medicine.[8]

For another example, in his book, *Heracles' Bow*, James Boyd White describes the centrality of story and narrative in the practice of the law:

> The language the lawyer uses and remakes is a language of meaning in the fullest sense. It is a language in which our perceptions of the natural universe are constructed and related, in which our values and motives are defined, in which our methods of reasoning are elaborated and enacted; and it gives us our terms for constructing a social universe by defining roles and actors and by establishing expectations as to the propriety of speech and conduct. Law always operates through speakers located in particular times and places speaking to actual audiences about real people. Its language is continuous with ordinary language; it always operates by narrative; it is not conceptual in its structure; it is perpetually reaffirmed or rejected in a social process; and it contains a system of internal translation by which it can reach a range of hearers.[9]

As he reminds his readers that the law begins and ends in ordinary language and ordinary experience, White also reminds his professional colleagues that the character of the practices of the law begins and ends in their presence, within their control. He argues that the professional responsibility of lawyers is to use language to realize their work in a manner appropriate to their finest conceptions of the law.

> [T]he law is what I have called culture-specific, that is, that it always takes place in a cultural context into which it is always an intervention. But it is in a similar way socially specific. . . . From this point of view the law can be

seen, as it is experienced, not as an independent system of meaning, but as a way of talking about real events and actual people in the world. At its heart it is a way of telling a story about what has happened in the world and claiming a meaning for it by writing an ending to it. The lawyer is repeatedly saying, or imagining himself or herself saying: "Here is 'what happened'; here is 'what it means'; and here is 'why it means what I claim.'" The process is at heart a narrative one because there cannot be a legal case without a real story about real people actually located in time and space and culture. Some actual person must go to a lawyer with an account of the experience upon which he or she wants the law to act, and the account will always be a narrative.

. . . This story will in the first instance be told in the language of its actors. That is where the law begins; in a sense this is also where it ends, for its object is to provide an ending to that story that will work in the world. And since the story both begins and ends in ordinary language and experience, the heart of the law is the process of translation by which it must work, from ordinary language to legal language and back again.[10]

Just as White argues that the practice of the law begins and ends in ordinary language and experience, I wish to argue that the practice of education must begin and end in ordinary language and experience. Just as White argues that "the heart of the law is the process of translation by which it must work, from ordinary language to legal language and back again," I wish to argue that the heart of education must be the process of translation by which it must work, from the explanations of their understandings that students explore with their teachers to discussions in which teachers explore the dynamics of learning and teaching with other educators and back again to enriched conversations between teachers and their students. Just as White argues that the professional responsibility of lawyers is to use language in such a way as to realize practices appropriate to their best conceptions of the law, I wish to argue that the professional responsibility of educators is to use language to realize practices appropriate to our best conceptions of learning and teaching.

The practice of education begins and ends in ordinary language and experience, in teachers' and students' dialogic exchanges and interactions with one another. To be beneficially influential, research in education must speak meaningfully to practicing teachers about their experiences with students. One way to ensure that this will be the case will be for practicing teachers to begin to speak in ordinary language about what they know, about what perplexes them about these experiences, and for the profession of education to recognize teachers' reflections and discussions as the publication of research, which the profession sorely requires.

Speculating on the potential benefit to his profession of thinking of the law as the realization of ordinary language and experience viewed from a legal perspective, White writes:

If, as I think, it is more true to the experience of those engaged in the activity of law than the standard conceptual accounts, it should in the first place lead to richer and more accurate teaching and practice of law and to a greater sense of control over what we do. Law might come to be seen as something that lawyers themselves make all the time, whenever they act as lawyers, not as something that is made by a political sovereign.[11]

If the practice of education were to be understood as beginning and ending with the ordinary language and experience of students and teachers working to make meaning at a particular time in a particular place, not as the enactment of curricula made by specialists beyond those classrooms, not as the transmission from teachers to students of a body of information, not as students' reproductions of information and procedures, this vision might lead to teachers and students having a greater sense of control over what they do and, therefore, to richer and more effective teaching and learning.

If research in education were understood as a way of telling a story about what happened in the world and claiming a meaning for that story by writing an ending to it, educators might find that teachers' stories have significant place and purpose in the body of knowledge that informs the work of the profession. We might even find in these stories a fresh view of the field.

Notes

1. Donald Schon, *The Reflective Practitioner.* (New York: Basic Books, 1983):31.

2. Schon, *The Reflective Practitioner,* 45.

3. For an essay that takes shape as a prosaic history of the teacher-research movement, as well as an extensive bibliography of the work of teachers of literacy who have conducted and published their research, see Cathy Fleischer, "Researching Teacher-research: A Practitioner's Retrospective," *English Education* (May, 1994): 86–124. The "Select Bibliography" at the end of this book references the works of teacher-researchers whose inquiries are increasingly informing the practice of teachers of literacy at all levels.

4. Kenneth Burke. *The Grammar of Motives.* (Berkeley, CA: University of California Press, 1969): 60.

5. Here I am claiming that teachers in the United States today who are conducting phenomenological research into their practice are working within their professional culture and our larger society, in both of which, as Jerome Bruner reminds us, narratives operate to forge "links between the exceptional and the ordinary." See *Acts of Meaning.* (Cambridge, MA: Harvard University Press, 1990):47.

The operant narratives of our professional culture and our society allow us teachers to make "happenings comprehensible against the background of ordinariness we take as the basic state of life" (Bruner, 96). As we focus attention on particular teaching-learning moments, trying to make sense of them, we do so within the larger sense-making systems in which we think, interpret and act, systems that are alive and well in the narratives of the cultures and the societies we inhabit. It is important to note that we researching teachers who rely on particular narratives to "render the exceptional comprehensible" (Bruner, 52) sometimes question the very narratives that guide our interpretations of occurrences. When we are unable to translate our anecdotes into events that have meaning and significance within the underlying plots and themes on which we rely to account for our experience, our anecdotes begin to reshape our larger narratives. The teacher-research movement itself can be described as a response to the failure of the narratives developed within various social science paradigms that have guided educational research to speak meaningfully and purposefully to education's practitioners.

6. Kathryn Montgomery Hunter. *Doctors' Stories: The Narrative Structure of Medical Knowledge*. (Princeton, NJ: Princeton University Press, 1991).

7. Hunter, *Doctors' Stories: The Narrative Structure of Medical Knowledge,* 76.

8. Hunter, *Doctors' Stories: The Narrative Structure of Medical Knowledge,* 74–75.

9. White, *Heracle's Bow,* 37.

10. White, *Heracle's Bow,* 35–36.

11. White, *Heracle's Bow,* 41.

Select Bibliography

Atwell, Nancie. *In the Middle: Writing, Reading, and Learning with Adolescents.* Portsmouth, NH: Boynton/Cook • Heinemann, 1987.

Bartholomae, David and Anthony Petrosky. *Facts, Artifacts, and Counterfacts.* Portsmouth, NH: Boynton/Cook • Heinemann, 1987.

Bakhtin, Mikhail. *The Dialogic Imagination.* Michael Holquist, ed. Caryl Emerson and Michael Holquist, trans. Austin, TX: University of Texas Press, 1981.

Bissex, Glenda L. and Richard Bullock, eds. *Seeing Ourselves: Case Study Research by Teachers of Writing.* Portsmouth, NH: Heinemann, 1987.

Branscombe, N., Amanda, Dixie Goswami, and Jeffrey Schwartz. *Students Teaching, Teachers Learning.* Portsmouth, NH: Boynton/Cook, 1982.

Brodkey, Linda. "On the Subjects of Class and Gender in 'The Literacy Letters,'" *College English.* 51:2 (Feb., 1989): 125–141.

Bruner, Jerome. *Acts of Meaning.* Cambridge, MA: Harvard University Press, 1990.

_____. *Actual Minds, Possible Worlds.* Cambridge, MA: Harvard University Press, 1986.

Burke, Kenneth. *The Grammar of Motives.* Berkeley, CA: University of California Press, 1969.

Cochran-Smith, Marilyn and Susan L. Lytle. "Research on Teaching and Teacher Research: The Issues that Divide," *Educational Researcher* 19 (1990): 2–11.

Cochran-Smith, Marilyn. *Inside/Outside: Teacher Research and Knowledge.* New York: Teachers College Press, 1993.

Csikszentmihalyi, Mihaly and Reed Larson, *Being Adolescent: Conflict and Growth in the Teenage Years,* New York: Basic Books, 1984.

Fleischer, Cathy. "Researching Teacher-research: A Practitioner's Retrospective," *English Education* (May, 1994): 86–124.

Freire, Paulo. The *Pedagogy of the Oppressed.* New York: The Continuum Publishing Corp., 1981.

Goodman, K. S. and Yetta Goodman. "Learning to Read is Natural." In *Theory and Practice of Early Reading,* vol. II., edited by L.B. Resnick and P.A. Weaver. Hillsdale, NJ: Erlbaum, 1979.

Goswami, Dixie. "Teachers as Researchers." In *Rhetoric and Composition: A Sourcebook for Teachers and Writers,* edited by Richard L. Graves. Upper Montclair, NJ: Boynton Cook, 1984: 347–358.

_____. and Peter Stillman, eds. *Reclaiming the Classroom: Teacher Research as an Agency for Change.* Portsmouth, NH: Boynton/Cook, 1984.

Greene, Maxine. *Landscapes of Learning*. New York: Teachers College Press, 1978.

Hallowell, Tommy, *Varsity Coach*. New York: Bantam, 1986.

Heath, Shirley Brice. *Ways with Words: Communities, Life, and Work in Communities and Classrooms*. New York: Cambridge University Press, 1983.

_____ and Charlene Thomas, "The Achievement of Preschool Literacy for Mother and Child." In *Awakening to Literacy*, edited by Hillel Goelman and Antoinette Oberg. London: Heinemann Educational Books, 1984: 51–72.

Hirsch, E. D. *Cultural Literacy: What Every American Needs to Know*. New York: Vintage Books, 1988.

Hunter, Kathryn Montgomery. *Doctors' Stories: The Narrative Structure of Medical Knowledge*. Princeton, NJ: Princeton University Press, 1991.

King, Stephen. "The Body." In *Different Seasons*. New York: New American Library, 1982: 289–436.

Knoblauch, C. H. and Lil Brannon. "Knowing Our Knowledge: A Phenomenological Basis for Teacher Research." In *Audits of Meaning: A Festschrift in Honor of Ann E. Berthoff*, edited by Louise Z. Smith. Portsmouth, NH: Boynton/Cook • Heinemann, 1988: 17–28.

Lloyd-Jones, Richard, and Andrea A. Lunsford, eds. *The English Coalition Conference: Democracy through Language*. Urbana, IL: NCTE, 1989.

Macrorie, Ken. *Searching Writing*. Upper Montclair, NJ: Boynton/Cook • Heinemann, 1984.

Meyrowitz, Joshua. "The Adultlike Child and the Childlike Adult: Socialization in an Electronic Age," *Daedalus: The Journal of the American Academy of Arts and Sciences*. (Summer, 1984):19–48.

Mohr, Marion M. and Marian S. Maclean. *Working Together: A Guide for Teacher-Researchers*. Urbana, IL: NCTE, 1987.

Myers, Miles. *The Teacher-Researcher: How to Study Writing in the Classroom*. Urbana, IL: NCTE, 1985.

Nixon, J. *A Teacher's Guide to Action Research*. London: Grant McIntyre, 1981.

North, Stephen M. *The Making of Knowledge in Composition: Portrait of an Emerging Field*. Upper Montclair, NJ: Boyton/Cook, 1987.

_____. "Writing in a Philosophy Class," *Research in the Teaching of English*. 20:3 (October, 1986): 225–262.

O'Neal, Zibby. *In Summer Light*. New York: Bantam, 1986.

Paley, V. G. *Wally's Stories: Conversations in Kindergarten*. Cambridge, MA.: Harvard University Press, 1981.

Piercy, Marge. "Unlearning not to speak." In *Circles on the Water*. New York: Alfred A. Knopf, 1994: 27.

Pinnell, Gay Su and M. L. Martin. *Teacher and Research: Language Learning in the Classroom*. Neward, DE: IRA, 1989.

Ray, Ruth. *The Practice of Theory: Teacher Research in Composition*. Urbana, IL: NCTE, 1993.

Rich, Adrienne, "Transcendental Etude." In *Lesbian Poetry,* edited by Elly Bulkin and Joan Larkin. Watertown, MS: Persephone Press, 1981: 16–20.

Robinson, Jay L. *Conversations on the Written Word.* Portsmouth, NH: Boynton/Cook, 1990.

_____. and Patricia Lambert Stock, "The Politics of Literacy." In Jay L. Robinson. *Conversations on the Written Word,* Portsmouth, NH: Boynton/Cook, 1990.

_____ and Bernard Van't Hul. *Real World English: Words; Real World English: Sentences; Real World English: Language Variation.* New York: Scholastic Books, 1978.

Rudduck, Jean and David Hopkins. *Research as a Basis for Teaching: Readings from the Work of Lawrence Stenhouse.* London: Heinemann Educational Books, 1985.

Schon, Donald. *The Reflective Practitioner.* New York: Basic Books, 1983.

Silko, Leslie Marmon. *Ceremony.* New York: New American Library, 1977.

Sizer, Theodore. *Horace's Compromise.* Boston: Houghton Mifflin, 1984.

Smith, Jenifer. "Setting the Cat Among the Pigeons: A Not So Sentimental Journey to the Heart of Teaching," *English Education* 23, 1991.

Sterling, Nora. *You Would If You Loved Me.* New York: Avon, 1982.

Stock, Patricia Lambert. "The Function of Anecdote in Teacher Research," *English Education* (Oct., 1993): 173–187.

_____. "The Rhetoric of Assessment," In *The Assessment of Learning: The 1991 ASCD Yearbook,* edited by Vito Perrone. Washington, DC: ASCD, 1991.

_____. "Taking on Testing: Chapter Two, " In *Hands on Assessment of Elementary School Science.,* edited by George E. Hein. Grand Forks, ND: North Dakota Study Group on Evaluation, 1990: 31–63.

Strassner, Todd. Angel *Dust Blues.* New York: Putnam, 1979.

White, James Boyd. *Heracles' Bow: Essays on the Rhetoric and Poetics of the Law.* Madison, WI: University of Wisconsin Press, 1985.

_____. *Justice as Translation: An Essay in Cultural and Legal Criticism.* Chicago: The University of Chicago Press, 1990.

_____. When *Words Lose Their Meaning.* Chicago: The University of Chicago Press, 1984.

Wigginton, Eliot. Some*times a Shining Moment: The Foxfire Experience.* New York: Anchor Press/Doubleday, 1986.

Please remember that this is a library book,
and that it belongs only temporarily to each
person who uses it. Be considerate. Do
not write in this, or any, library book.